CROSS STITCH
FLOWER GARDENS

CROSS STITCH
FLOWER GARDENS
FROM 2 HOURS TO 2 WEEKS

CHRISTINA MARSH

David & Charles

746.443
MAR

A DAVID & CHARLES BOOK

VWM ES VWM

First published in the UK in 1998

Text and designs Copyright © Christina Marsh 1998
Photography and layout Copyright © David & Charles 1998

Christina Marsh has asserted her right to be identified as author of this work
in accordance with the Copyright, Designs and Patents Act, 1988.

The designs in this book are copyright and must not be stitched for resale.

All rights reserved. No part of this publication may be reproduced, stored
in a retrieval system, or transmitted, in any form or by any means, electronic
or mechanical, by photocopying, recording or otherwise, without prior
permission in writing from the publisher.

A catalogue record for this book is available from the British Library.

ISBN 0 7153 0611 1

Page 2 (clockwise from left): *Pansy-pot Gloves (page 24), Floral Wheelbarrow Card (page 28),
Cottage Garden Picture (page 30), Pansy Gift Tag (page 20), Pansy Key Ring (page 21),
Pansy Greetings Card (page 23) and Seed Packet Holder (page 26)*

Photography by Christina Marsh
Watercolours by Christina Marsh
Poems by Elizabeth Marsh
Line drawings by Ethan Danielson
Applemac design by Kit Johnson with
Dorchester Typesetting Group Ltd.

Printed in Great Britain by Butler & Tanner Ltd
for David & Charles
Brunel House Newton Abbot Devon

CONTENTS

INTRODUCTION

As a keen gardener it gave me great pleasure to have the opportunity to create the cross stitch gardens featured in this book. It was also challenging, for I had to find the correct plants for each of the gardens featured. I now have a much wider knowledge of where many of my favourite plants come from and realize that my own garden is a happy mixture of different garden styles.

The eight garden designs incorporated in this book have been chosen for their contrasting styles and a special colour scheme has been created for each of them. If you like strong, vibrant colours then the rich golden yellows and deep reds of the Japanese Garden will appeal to you. If, however, you are drawn to pastel colour schemes you may prefer the pale peach tones of the Rose Garden or the mixture of pink and lilac tones in the Herb Garden. With so many different gardens and colour schemes to choose from you are spoilt for choice.

The projects in this book cater for all skill levels and are particularly suitable for beginners. Each chapter has a co-ordinated gift set which has been designed with the beginner in mind. All the projects have been graded according to skill level and these are listed in an easy-to-use chart at the beginning of this book.

The projects have also been graded according to stitching time and four time grades have been developed. The two hour and two day projects have been especially created for the beginner, although some of the one week projects are also for beginners. Most of the one week projects are for stitchers with some experience whilst the gardens are for the more experienced stitchers. Whatever your skill level, you will find plenty of projects tailor-made for you.

You will also see that many of the projects are adaptable. For instance, all the gift tag designs will make key rings or pictures which can be framed in a trinket box lid. Further ideas are given at the beginning of each chapter, and the section entitled Creative Options on page 13 will show you how to adapt threads and fabric to create your own colour schemes and how to reduce or enlarge designs by changing the fabric. This book offers endless creative choices.

I hope you will derive as much pleasure from stitching these projects as I had in designing them. Happy stitching!

Clockwise from top: *Herb Garden Picture (page 100), Lavender Greetings Card (page 92), Lavender Gift Tag (page 90) and Lavender Sachet (page 93)*

BASIC TECHNIQUES

The quick-reference guide given for each embroidery project is an easy-to-use set of instructions for the more experienced embroiderer. If you are a beginner, or trying a new technique for the first time, you will find the following in-depth instructions helpful.

Finding the centre of the fabric
Find the centre of the fabric by folding the material in half and then in half again, then lightly pressing it. Open out the fabric and run one vertical and one horizontal line of tacking (basting) along the creased folds. Do not cross stitch over the tacking (basting) because you will find it difficult to remove later. Instead, cut away the tacking (basting) as you stitch. If you intend to place your work in a square or rectangular frame, leave the tacking (basting) at the outer edges of the fabric – these lines will help you centre the embroidery on the backing card when you come to frame it.

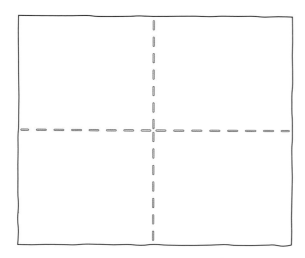

Marking the centre of the fabric

Mounting work in a circular frame
Embroidery hoops come in a wide range of sizes and consist of two rings, one fitted inside the other. The outer ring usually has a

screw attachment for tightening the frame. To mount fabric in an embroidery hoop first remove the outer ring. Place the fabric over the inner ring and secure it by placing the outer ring over the fabric so that the material is trapped between the two hoops. Tighten the screw to secure the fabric. The embroidery should be removed from the hoop between sewing sessions because the frame may mark the fabric.

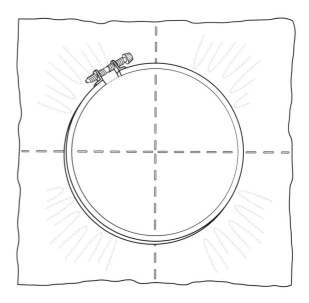

Working in a hoop

Mounting work in a rectangular frame
A rectangular frame is more suited to larger projects such as the garden pictures. Slate frames come in a variety of sizes but you will only need a small frame for the projects in this book. Before cutting out the fabric always make sure it is wide enough to fit the

frame. To mount the fabric first pin one side of the material to the tape on one roller. Stitch the fabric to the tape and remove the pins. Repeat this operation on the other side. The shorter sides of the fabric are laced to the sides of the frame with strong thread as shown in the diagram below.

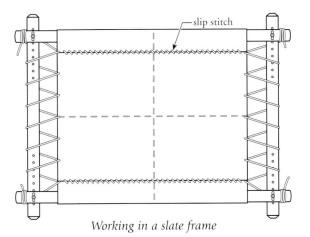

Working in a slate frame

Tacking (basting)

Working from left to right, run the needle in and out of the fabric to make long, evenly spaced stitches.

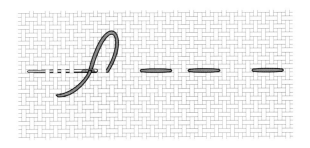

Working tacking (basting) stitches

Cross stitch

Form a single cross stitch by taking a diagonal stitch as shown in the diagram (top right). Draw the needle out of the bottom right-hand hole and take a second diagonal stitch over the top to form a cross. Large areas of cross stitches can be worked in rows, making a series of diagonal stitches in one direction before returning to cross them. If you wish to

check you are doing this correctly, turn your work over – the stitching at the back should form rows of straight stitches.

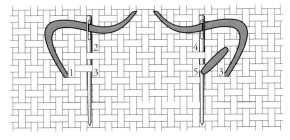

Working a single cross stitch

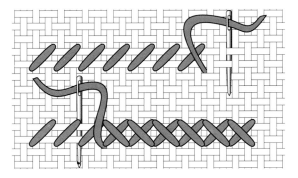

Working rows of cross stitches

Backstitch

Backstitch is used for all the outline work. The stitch is worked from left to right. Bring the needle up and take it back into the fabric one square to the right of the starting point. Then pass it below the fabric and bring it up one square to the left of the stitch. By repeating this action you produce a line which can be taken in any direction.

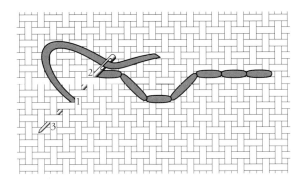

Backstitching

Longstitch

A longstitch is formed by a single stitch which may be taken over several squares. Draw the needle through the hole at the starting point for the line and insert it at the finishing point for the line, creating one long stitch. Take extra care securing the knot when stitching with one strand of thread.

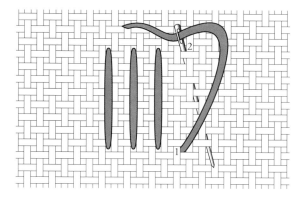

Working longstitch

Satin stitch

This stitch is used to cover an area completely with thread. In this book it is used for the well rope in the Wild Flower Picture. To work the stitch, take parallel long stitches which butt up together. The stitches may be the same length or graded.

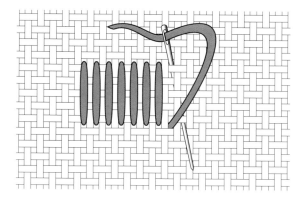

Working satin stitch

French knots

Bring the thread through the fabric at the required position and wind it once or twice round the needle (see above right). Insert the

needle slightly to the side of the emerging thread and pull the needle through. Take care neither to allow the thread to slacken nor pull too tight. Knot the thread on the back or go on to work the next stitch. Practise stitches on a scrap of fabric before working them on your embroidery.

Adding French knots

Slip stitch

Slip stitching is used for hemming and finishing off openings. The stitching is usually worked in ordinary sewing cotton with a sharp needle. Bring the needle through one layer of fabric and insert it in the second layer, bringing it back out in the first layer as shown in the diagram below. By repeating this movement a line of fairly close diagonal stitches is formed running from right to left.

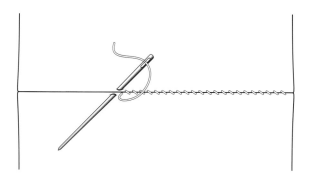

Slip stitching

Waste canvas

Waste canvas is used for cross stitching on fabrics other than evenweave. The canvas comes in a variety of counts but you will only need 14 count for the projects in this book. Waste canvas looks similar to tapestry canvas but it is prised away when the embroidery is complete.

Using waste canvas

Pin the canvas in position on the fabric (the pins can be removed after a few stitches have secured the canvas to the fabric). Work the cross stitches with a sharp needle, passing it through the canvas holes and into the fabric. On completion, dampen the canvas to release the size, and use tweezers to remove the waste canvas threads one by one. This job requires patience and can't be rushed.

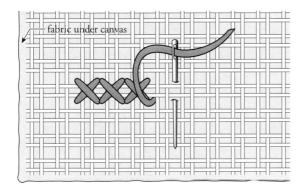

Working on waste canvas

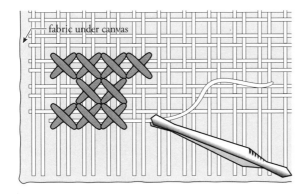

Removing canvas threads

Mounting work on card for a frame

First prepare the mounting card by drawing two central lines with a pencil and ruler on the back of the card. Attach the wadding (batting) to the front of the card by spreading a thin layer of glue over the surface and gently pressing the wadding (batting) on top. Allow the glue to dry.

Place the embroidery face down and lay the padded side of the board face down on top. Use the tacking (basting) lines to help centre the embroidery by aligning them with the pencil lines on the back of the card (see the diagram below).

Turn the corners (as shown) and use masking tape to secure them temporarily. Turn in the side flaps and lace the work with a strong thread, running it backwards and forwards across the back and firmly pulling the surplus material tightly over the backing board. Repeat this operation with the top and bottom flaps. Oversew the mitred corners and remove any tacking remaining on the right side of the work. It is not necessary to lace a small picture – the four flaps can be secured with masking tape or fabric glue.

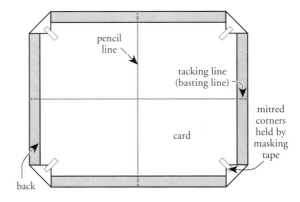

Mounting your work

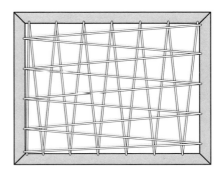

Lacing the edges together

Mounting work in a flexi-frame

A flexi-frame is similar to an embroidery hoop: it consists of an outer ring with a hanging loop at the top and a smaller inner ring which fits inside. This type of frame comes in a range of different colours and a variety of different shapes and sizes.

Before mounting your work, remove the tacking (basting) stitches. Place the embroidery right-side up over the inner ring, making sure the design is centred. Place the outer ring over the embroidery, trapping the fabric between the two rings. It can be difficult stretching the outer hoop over the inner ring and you may find a second pair of hands helpful for this task.

Turn the frame to the back and trim the surplus material, leaving approximately 12 mm (½ in) around the edge of the frame. Use a strong thread to run a line of running stitches around the edge and draw the thread until the fabric pulls in towards the centre back of the frame. Knot and fasten the thread end securely.

To finish off the back cut a circular disc of white felt slightly smaller than the aperture of the flexi-frame. Place the felt over the back opening and slip stitch it neatly in place around the edge with white cotton. (If you have used white Aida do not use a coloured felt for the backing as this will show through on the right side.)

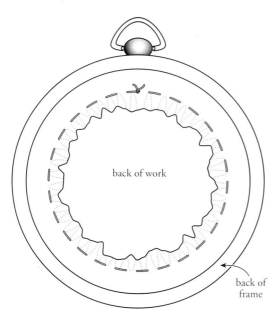

Gathering up the edges

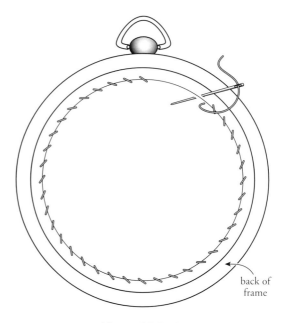

Adding a felt backing

GETTING STARTED

Everything you need to know to work the projects in this book is in this chapter –
from which fabrics and threads to use to which projects to choose. So, whether you are a beginner
or an experienced stitcher, do read this section first.

CHOOSING THE RIGHT PROJECT

The unique approach of this book lets you choose a project that is right for you, whatever your ability and whatever time you've got. All the projects in this book are graded according to the skill required to stitch and assemble the item. So if you are a beginner check the skill level of a project before starting work. The table on page 17 will help you. Each chapter contains at least three beginner's projects as part of the co-ordinated gift set.

You will find that cross stitching is an enjoyable and easy skill to acquire and if you are a beginner you will soon grow in proficiency and develop the confidence to tackle the more advanced projects in this book – not just the intermediate projects but also the more difficult pictures.

FINDING TIME TO STITCH

I have graded all the projects according to the time it takes to stitch them, so you will know if you can complete one in the time you have available. However, it is impossible to state precisely how long a project will take to stitch as much will depend on experience and the pace at which you work. For example: an embroidery listed as a one week project is based on a stitcher with average skill who has at least two hours to stitch each day.

If you are a beginner you may find that your initial projects take longer to stitch, but don't worry – the main thing is that you enjoy the stitching. As you grow in skill and confidence you will find that you begin to stitch faster.

CREATIVE OPTIONS

I have specified the colours and fabrics to use for every project so you can reproduce them exactly, but do feel free to adapt the colour schemes if you wish. Here are some pointers to help you.

CHOOSING THE RIGHT FABRICS

Most of the projects have been stitched on 14 count Aida because this is an easy-to-

stitch fabric, especially suitable for beginners. If you are a more experienced stitcher you may wish to use an evenweave or linen fabric, in which case you can replace the Aida with a 28-count evenweave fabric.

You can also alter the finished size of your design by changing the count. The count of a fabric refers to how many holes there are in every 2.5cm (1in). (Although we buy lengths

Above Stitching on fabrics of different counts will affect the size of the design. This geranium has been stitched on, from left to right, 11-, 14- and 18-count Aida. You may also need to adjust the number of strands you work with.

of fabric in metres and centimetres, counts are still calculated in holes per inch by manufacturers – even by those in countries where they use metric measurements in daily life. A strange anomaly!)

Try stitching a design on fabrics of different counts and you will find that the size of the design changes. As the count lowers there are fewer stitches to the inch, therefore the design is larger. Conversely the higher the hole count the smaller the stitch and the number of stitches to the inch increases, with the result that the work is smaller (see above).

Changing the count is an easy option but you must also remember to change the number of strands you stitch with. Use more strands with lower-count fabrics. The quick-reference table below gives the number of strands to use for each fabric count.

COUNT	FABRIC	CROSS STITCH	BACKSTITCH
11	Aida	Three strands	Two strands
14	Aida	Two strands	One strand
16	Aida	One/two strands	One strand
18	Aida	One strand	One strand
22	Evenweave	Three strands	Two strands
28	Linen	Two strands	One strand

COLOUR OPTIONS

As well as changing the size, you can also change the colour of your fabric. You will find the largest variety in 14-count Aida fabrics, and less choice in the higher or lower thread counts.

The background colour will affect the tonal quality of your work. For example: if you stitch on green or blue fabric the colour of the threads will be subdued, whilst the same design stitched on white or cream may appear much brighter. If you wish to stitch on a darker background but want to maintain the same colour density add an extra strand of cotton to the recommended number of stitching threads.

It is not difficult to change the colour scheme of a design, although I would not recommend this for beginners. I suggest you start with a small design, such as the pansy shown in the picture overleaf. Use graph paper and coloured pencils to copy the

Above Colours look brighter and more vivid on cream or white fabrics than on deeper tones, so take this into account when buying your threads.

Above *Change the colour of your threads to give a design a whole new look. However, make sure you keep darker and lighter colours in the same relative positions.*

design in your new colours so you can see if you like the effect. When you are happy with it, you will be able to use your drawing as your colour key chart.

It is important when substituting a new range of colours to shade your design in a similar way to the original. With the pansy design, for example, the three main petals in each colourway are made of two shades of the same colour. The darker shade is always on the outer edge and the lighter shade is used nearer the centre. Here, the lower back petals are shown in a dark colour and this has been repeated in each colourway.

If you change the colour of a flower you may also need to alter the shade of the foliage. In the case of the blue pansy I have changed the centre colour from green to yellow because I felt that the effect was too flat with green in the middle. If you keep to these basic rules you will find that changing a colour scheme is a simple task.

SKILL AND TIME RATINGS

All the projects have been graded according to the skill level and the time they take to work. The time allocations are based on a stitcher with average ability, stitching for two hours per day. Experienced stitchers may find it easier to complete the projects within the time allowed, whilst a beginner may take slightly longer to finish the same projects.

Use the table opposite as a rough guide to skill and time requirements. The skill level is indicated by the star rating. Beginner projects have a one star rating and projects for stitchers with some experience have two stars. The three star rating indicates projects suitable for experienced stitchers. Projects with dual ratings are suitable for both levels.

TWO-HOUR PROJECTS

Geranium Gift Tag	★
Water-Lily Gift Tag	★
Lavender Gift Tag	★
Rose Gift Tag	★
Pansy Gift Tag	★
Periwinkle Gift Tag	★
Cactus Gift Tag	★
Azalea Gift Tag	★
Rose Handkerchief	★/★★
Pansy Key Ring	★/★★
Azalea Trinket Box	★/★★

TWO-DAY PROJECTS

Water-Lily Card	★
Water-Lily Picture	★
Cactus Picture	★
Cactus Card	★
Pansy Card	★
Geranium Card	★
Geranium Magnet	★
Protea Picture	★
Lavender Card	★
Lavender Sachet	★/★★
Bergamot Key Ring	★/★★
Rose Card	★/★★
Periwinkle Card	★/★★
Periwinkle Coaster	★/★★
Azalea Card	★/★★
Rose Napkin	★★★
Pansy Gloves	★★★

ONE-WEEK GIFT SETS

Water-Lily Set	★
Geranium Set	★
Pansy Set	★
Cacti Set	★
Lavender Set	★/★★
Periwinkle Set	★/★★
Rose Set	★/★★
Azalea Set	★/★★

ONE-WEEK PROJECTS

Colourful Pot Covers	★
Floral Wheelbarrow Card	★
Iris Pin Cushion	★/★★
Iris Scissors' Case	★/★★
Bergamot Card	★/★★
Bergamot Bag	★/★★
Gazanias Picture	★★
Temple Picture	★★
Golden Lilies Hanging	★★
Wild Flower Bookmark	★★
Wild Flower Book Cover	★★★
Pansy Seed Packet Holder	★★★
Rose Table Mat	★★★

TWO-WEEK PROJECTS

Rose Garden Picture	★★
Herb Garden Picture	★★
Tropical Garden Picture	★★/★★★
Japanese Garden Picture	★★/★★★
Water Garden Picture	★★/★★★
Mediterranean Garden Picture	★★/★★★
Cottage Garden Picture	★★/★★★
Wild Flower Garden Picture	★★/★★★

THE
COTTAGE
GARDEN

It's the informality of the cottage garden that most appeals to me, and my own pocket-sized garden leans in this direction. It has taken many years of hard work to turn my dream garden into reality and I am still busy adding to it each year. Fortunately, creating these embroideries based on the cottage garden will be much quicker and simpler than trying to create the real thing. I have chosen pansies as my main flowers for this chapter because their bright colourful markings make them a pleasure to stitch.

I pause in pleasure at the garden gate,
Inhaling the vision that my eyes await.
Hollyhocks rise by the rust-gilded latch,
As I pass on through to the pansy patch.

*M*eandering through a leafy glade,
I follow a path to the summerhouse shade
Where wisteria fronds climb and run
And geranium blooms bask in the sun.

PANSY GIFT TAG

Project time: TWO HOURS

A pretty pansy is the perfect motif for a summer gift tag, and it can be produced in an evening.

Skill level: BEGINNER

14-count white Aida, 7.5 cm (3 in) square

Tacking thread

Sewing needle

No 26 tapestry needle

One skein of stranded embroidery cotton (floss) in each of the colours shown in the chart

Gift tag with a 3.5 cm (1⅜ in) circular or square aperture

Solid glue stick

● These instructions are a quick-reference guide for this project. For more detailed information see Basic Techniques, page 8.

1. Mark the centre of the fabric with one vertical and one horizontal line of tacking (basting). This design can be worked either hand-held or placed in a frame.

2. Start the embroidery in the centre of the fabric and cross stitch the design, following the chart and using two strands of embroidery cotton (floss).

3. Outline the pansy petals in backstitch with one strand of plum thread as indicated in the chart.

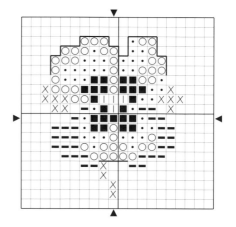

4. When you have finished the embroidery, trim surplus material leaving a 12 mm (½ in) border all round the design. The trimmed work should be approximately 2.5 cm (1 in) larger than the aperture.

5. Spread glue evenly on the mounting flap (you can see this through the aperture when the card is closed). Place the embroidery in position and lightly press the work and the front of the card to secure.

PANSY KEY RING

Project time: TWO HOURS

You'll take extra care of your keys when they're attached to this delightful pansy key ring, and the bold pansy flower should be easy to keep track of. If you wish you can turn any of the gift tag designs into key rings too.

Skill level: BEGINNER/IMPROVER

18-count white Aida, 7.5 cm (3 in) square (you will need more fabric if you wish to work the design in a frame)

Tacking thread

Sewing needle

No 26 tapestry needle

One skein of stranded embroidery cotton (floss) in each of the colours shown in the chart

Key ring with a 3 cm (1¼ in) circular aperture

● These instructions are a quick-reference guide for this project. For more detailed information see Basic Techniques, page 8.

1. Mark the centre of the fabric with one vertical and one horizontal line of tacking (basting). This design can be worked either hand-held or placed in a frame.

2. Start the embroidery in the centre of the fabric and cross stitch the design, following the chart and using one strand of thread.

3. Outline the pansy in backstitch with one strand of purple thread.

4. Trim the embroidery to fit the key ring aperture and assemble it, following the manufacturer's instructions.

PANSY GIFT TAG *(left)* & **KEY RING** *(right)*

		ANCHOR	DMC	MADEIRA
·	Lemon yellow	295	726	0109
○	Golden yellow	306	725	0113
−	Plum	59	600	0704
■	Navy blue	150	823	1008
		Medium green	225	703	1307
✕	Dark green	227	701	1305
+	Light blue	140	813	0909
●	Purple	102	550	0714

Backstitch outline
Pansy (gift tag): One strand of plum
Pansy (key ring): One strand of purple

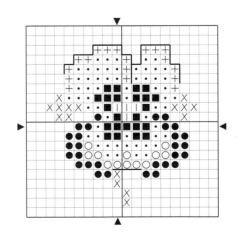

PANSY GREETINGS CARD

Project time: TWO DAYS

The smiling pansies on this card will light up the face of the recipient.

Skill level: BEGINNER

14-count white Aida, 12.5 cm (5 in) square (you will need more fabric if you wish to work your design in a frame)

Tacking thread

Sewing needle

No 26 tapestry needle

One skein of stranded embroidery cotton (floss) in each of the colours given in the panel

Card with a 6.5 cm (2½ in) circular aperture

Solid glue stick

● These instructions are a quick-reference guide for this project. For more detailed information see Basic Techniques, page 8.

Opposite These colourful pansy-covered items can be worked together in one week to make a gift set

1. Mark the centre of the fabric with one vertical and one horizontal line of tacking (basting). This design can be worked either hand-held or placed in a frame.

PANSY CARD *(below)*

		ANCHOR	DMC	MADEIRA
·	Lemon yellow	295	726	0109
○	Golden yellow	306	725	0113
+	Light blue	140	813	0909
■	Navy blue	150	823	1008
●	Purple	102	550	0714
−	Plum	59	600	0704
I	Medium green	225	703	1307
X	Dark green	227	701	1305

Backstitch outline
Blue/yellow pansies: One strand of purple
Yellow/plum pansy: One strand of plum

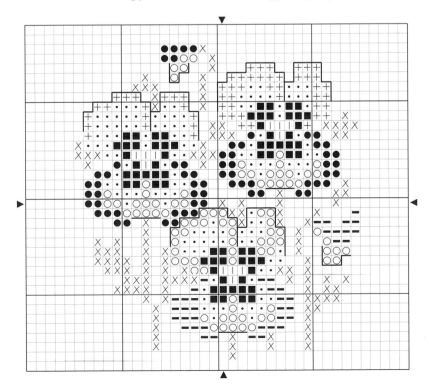

2. Start the embroidery in the centre of the fabric and cross stitch the design, following the chart and using two strands of embroidery cotton (floss).

3. Outline the blue/yellow pansies in backstitch with one strand of purple thread; to outline the yellow/plum pansy use one strand of plum thread.

4. Trim the surplus material leaving a 12 mm (½ in) border all round the design. Your work should be 9 cm (3½ in) square.

5. Open the card and spread glue evenly on the mounting flap (you can see this through the aperture when the card is closed). Place the embroidery in position and lightly press on the closed card to secure.

PANSY-POT GLOVES

Project time: TWO DAYS

With these colourful pansy motifs on your garden gloves, there'll be no keeping you away from the flowerbeds, whatever the season.

Skill level: EXPERIENCED

Two pieces of waste canvas, 7.5 cm (3 in) square

Garden gloves

Sharp pointed needle and pins

One skein of stranded embroidery cotton (floss) in each of the colours given in the panel

Tweezers

● These instructions are a quick-reference guide for this project. For more detailed information see Basic Techniques, page 8. For specific instructions on using waste canvas see page 11.

1. Arrange a square of canvas on each glove and pin it in place. (The pins can be removed after you've stitched the first few crosses.)

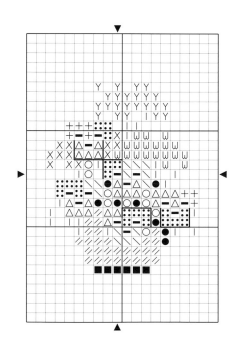

PANSY-POT GLOVES *(left)*

		ANCHOR	DMC	MADEIRA
╲	Lemon yellow	295	726	0109
△	Golden yellow	306	725	0113
✕	Light pink	55	962	0612
Y	Medium pink	57	309	0611
ш	Plum	59	600	0704
∷	Light blue	140	813	0909
+	Medium blue	142	799	0911
−	Navy blue	150	823	1008
I	Medium green	225	703	1307
O	Dark green	227	701	1305
●	Very dark green	246	395	1405
╱	Medium brown	944	433	2106
■	Dark brown	380	838	1914

Backstitch outline
Pansies: One strand of navy blue

Above Practical and pretty, these pansy-pot gloves will only take about two days to stitch

2. Work the design from the centre using three strands of thread. Be careful not to split the waste canvas when stitching as this will make the threads harder to remove and could spoil the look of your embroidery.

3. Outline the pansies in backstitch using one strand of navy thread.

4. Dampen the threads with a sponge to help release the size that holds the waste canvas rigid. Use a pair of tweezers to remove the threads individually; this requires patience and shouldn't be rushed.

SEED PACKET HOLDER

Project time: ONE WEEK

Store your seeds in style using this smart fabric holder which features a barrow-load of country flowers. Beginners can work this design for a card (see page 28).

Skill level: EXPERIENCED

Cotton fabric, 25 x 15 cm (10 x 6 in)

Medium-weight iron-on interfacing, 25 x 15 cm (10 x 6 in)

Bias binding, 25 x 2.5 cm (10 x 1 in)

14-count waste canvas, 11.5 x 10 cm (4½ x 4 in)

No 26 tapestry needle

One skein of stranded embroidery cotton (floss) in each of the colours given in the panel

Pins

Tweezers

Sharp needle

Sewing cotton

● Read all the instructions carefully before starting this project.
● These instructions are a quick-reference guide for this project. For more detailed information see Basic Techniques, page 8. For specific instructions on using waste canvas see page 11.

1. Place the interfacing, glue side down, on the back of the cotton fabric and press lightly with an iron to fuse.

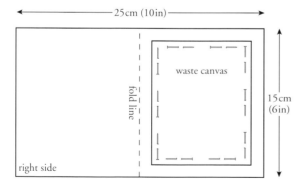

Positioning the waste canvas

2. Turn the fabric to the right side, fold it in half to find the centre, then unfold and pin the waste canvas on the right-hand side of the fabric, as shown in the diagram below left. The canvas should be positioned approximately 12 mm (½ in) from the side and bottom edges.

3. Find the centre. This should be simple because most waste canvas is marked with an easy-to-count grid.

4. Cross stitch the design from the centre, following the chart and using three strands of embroidery cotton (floss).

5. When you have completed the cross stitching, outline the pansies in backstitch using two strands of navy thread.

6. Remove the pins and trim surplus canvas leaving approximately 12 mm (½ in) all round the design.

7. Dampen the canvas with a sponge to release the glue, then remove the canvas threads one by one with tweezers. This requires patience – if you try to remove too many strands at once you could spoil the embroidery.

8. When you have removed all the waste canvas lightly press the design, protecting the work with a pressing cloth.

9. Open one side of the bias binding and place it on the top edge of the fabric; pin it in

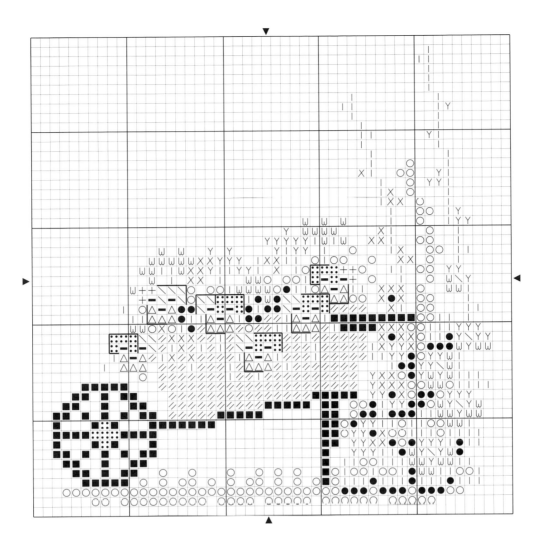

FLORAL WHEELBARROW
SEED PACKET HOLDER AND CARD *(above)*

		ANCHOR	DMC	MADEIRA
⧅	Lemon yellow	295	726	0109
△	Golden yellow	306	725	0113
⋰	Light blue	140	813	0909
+	Medium blue	142	799	0911
▬	Navy blue	150	823	1008
✕	Light pink	55	962	0612
Y	Medium pink	57	309	0611
⊍	Plum	59	600	0704
I	Medium green	225	703	1307
○	Dark green	227	701	1305
●	Very dark green	246	395	1405
⧄	Medium brown	944	433	2106
■	Dark brown	380	838	1914

Backstitch outline
Pansies on seed packet holder: Two strands of
navy blue
Pansies on card: One strand of navy blue

position. Machine or carefully hand-sew along the fold line. Turn the bias binding to the right side.

10. Fold the fabric in half and machine down the side and along the bottom, approximately 12 mm (½ in) from the edge of the material. Trim the surplus material from the seams and overlock the edge.

11. While the work is still inside-out, turn the bias binding to the back and slip stitch to secure. Turn the work to the right side and lightly press.

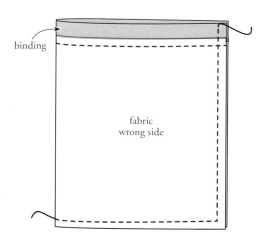

Stitching the seams

FLORAL WHEELBARROW CARD

Project time: ONE WEEK

Hollyhocks, pansies and other cottage-garden flowers explode from a floral greeting that can be made in a week but will last forever.

Skill level: BEGINNER

14-count yellow Aida, 15 cm (6 in) square (you will need more fabric if you wish to work the design in a frame)

Tacking thread

Sewing needle

No 26 tapestry needle

One skein of stranded embroidery cotton (floss) in each of the colours given in the panel

Card with a 10 cm (4 in) square aperture

Solid glue stick

● These instructions are a quick-reference guide for this project. For more detailed information see Basic Techniques, page 8.

1. Mark the centre of the fabric with one vertical and one horizontal line of tacking (basting). This design can be worked either hand-held or placed in a frame.

2. Start the embroidery in the centre of the fabric and cross stitch the design, following the chart and using two strands of embroidery cotton (floss).

3. Outline the pansies in backstitch with one strand of navy thread.

4. When you have finished the embroidery, trim surplus material leaving a 12 mm (½ in) border all round the design. Your trimmed work should measure 12.5 cm (5 in) square.

5. Open the card and spread glue evenly onto the mounting flap (you can see this through the aperture when the card is closed). Place the embroidery in position and lightly press the closed card to secure.

Opposite Use the same design (page 27) to make this charming seed packet holder and card.

Cottage Garden Picture

Project time: TWO WEEKS

Enjoy the secret delights of a garden that flowers in an eternal summer by making this super cross-stitch picture. With the summerhouse in the distance and hollyhocks growing round the gate, it could be the garden you've always dreamed of.

Skill level: IMPROVER/EXPERIENCED

14-count white Aida, 25.5 x 20cm (10 x 8in) rectangle

Tacking thread and thread to match the ring

Sewing needle

Embroidery frame

No 26 tapestry needle

One skein of stranded embroidery cotton (floss) in each of the colours given in the panel

6mm (¼ in) ring for the gate latch

Firm card, 17.5 x 12.5 cm (7 x 5 in)

Lightweight wadding (batting), 17.5 x 12.5 cm (7 x 5 in)

Solid glue stick

Strong thread for lacing

Frame with a 17.5 x 12.5 cm (7 x 5 in) internal aperture

● The ring shown is the catch from an old necklace

● These instructions are a quick-reference guide for this project. For more detailed information see Basic Techniques, page 8. For specific instructions on mounting the picture in a frame see pages 11-12.

1. Mark the centre of the fabric with one vertical and one horizontal line of tacking (basting). Place the prepared fabric in an embroidery frame.

2. Start the embroidery in the centre of the fabric and cross stitch the design, following the chart and using two strands of embroidery cotton (floss).

3. Complete all the cross stitching, then outline the embroidery in backstitch. Use two strands of cream thread to outline the bricks.

4. Remove the embroidery from the frame, hand wash it if necessary (using detergent suitable for delicates), and lightly press the work with a steam iron on the wrong side.

5. Attach the ring to the top right-hand side of the gate (see photograph on pages 30-31) by oversewing it using matching brown sewing thread.

6. Spread glue evenly on one side of the firm card and lightly press the wadding (batting) on top.

7. Centre the embroidery over the padded card and secure it on the back by lacing the edges together.

8. Finally, mount the picture in the frame, following the manufacturer's instructions.

COTTAGE GARDEN PICTURE (right)

		ANCHOR	DMC	MADEIRA
—	Cream	361	738	2013
••	Lemon yellow	295	726	0109
△	Golden yellow	306	725	0113
◇	Light blue	140	813	0909
3	Medium blue	142	799	0911
/	Light pink	55	962	0612
+	Medium pink	57	309	0611
⊔	Plum	59	600	0704
·	Light green	240	368	1209
I	Medium green	225	703	1307
O	Dark green	227	701	1305
●	Very dark green	246	395	1405
▢	Light brown	374	420	2104
U	Medium brown	944	433	2106
■	Dark brown	380	838	1914

Backstitch outline
Bricks: Two strands of cream

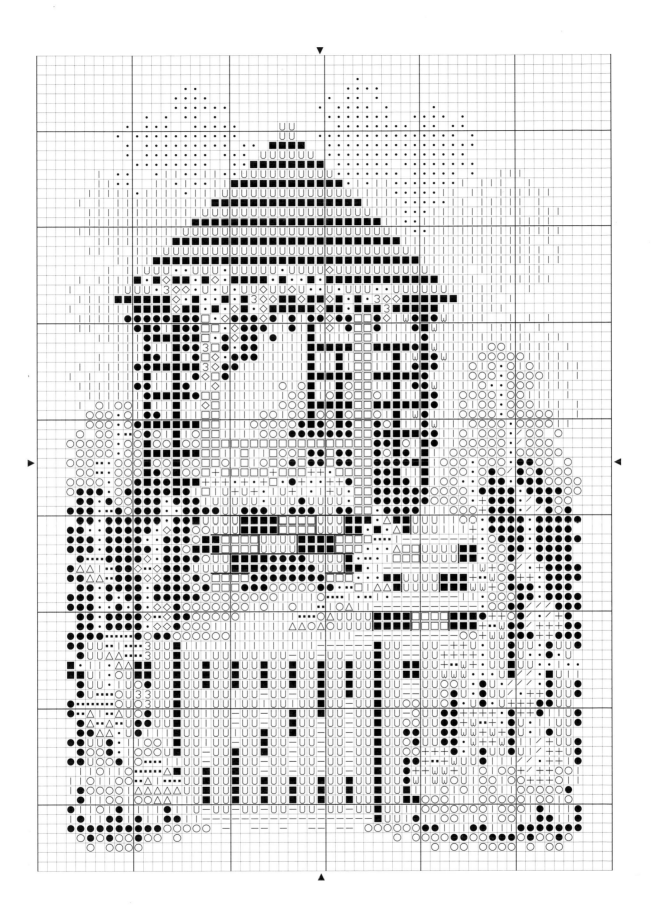

THE WATER GARDEN

Water gardens take many forms – from stately lakes to humble garden ponds. Some boast elegant fountains, some have tinkling streams while others are still. For my water garden I've chosen a waterfall leading to a lily pond to capture water both flowing and at rest. Stitch the designs for the projects shown or adapt them – the iris pin cushion would make a pretty scented sachet or a card.

How fast the water rushes – how quick,
Splashing the rhododendron bed.
How swift it moves, how clear and bright,
Reflecting petals of yellow and red!

How still is the pool the water reaches,
Where the irises stand so tall.
How lovely is this resting place,
With water lilies scented and cool.

WATER-LILY GIFT TAG

Project time: TWO HOURS

Make this pretty gift tag to go with an extra-special gift, or frame it to make a mini picture.

Skill level: BEGINNER

14-count pale blue Aida, 7.5 cm (3 in) square (you will need more fabric if you wish to work the design in a frame)

Tacking thread

Sewing needle

No 26 tapestry needle

One skein of stranded embroidery cotton (floss) in each of the colours shown in the chart

Gift tag with a 3 cm (1¼ in) square aperture

Solid glue stick

● These instructions are a quick-reference guide for this project. For more detailed information see Basic Techniques, page 8.

1. Mark the centre of the fabric with tacking (basting). This design can be worked either hand-held or placed in a frame.

2. Start the embroidery in the centre of the fabric and cross stitch the design, following the chart on page 38 and using two strands of thread.

3. Outline the design with backstitch using one strand of deep red thread.

4. Trim surplus material leaving 12 mm (½ in) all round the design. The trimmed work should be approximately 2.5 cm (1 in) larger than the aperture.

5. Spread glue evenly on the mounting flap (you can see this flap through the aperture when the card is closed). Place the finished embroidery in position and lightly press.

Opposite *Together the water-lily picture, gift tag and card can be worked in one week to produce this gift set*

WATER-LILY PICTURE

Project time: TWO DAYS

Unfurling water-lily flowers in shades of peach and red nestle in their bold green leaves in this engaging picture. The colours stand out well against the pale blue Aida which represents the cool water of the pond.

Skill level: BEGINNER

14-count pale blue Aida, 15.5 cm (6 in) square (you will need more fabric if you wish to work the design in a frame)

Tacking thread

Sewing needle

No 26 tapestry needle

One skein of stranded embroidery cotton (floss) in each of the colours shown in the chart

Cotton backing fabric, 12.5 cm (5 in) square

5 cm (2 in) circular flexi-frame

Pale blue sewing thread

● These instructions are a quick-reference guide for this project. For more detailed information see Basic Techniques, page 8. See page 12 for details on mounting your finished work in a flexi-frame.

1. Mark the centre of the fabric with one vertical and one horizontal line of tacking (basting). This design can be worked either hand-held or placed in a frame.

2. Start the embroidery in the centre of the fabric and cross stitch the design, following the chart and using two strands of thread.

3. Outline the flowers and leaves in backstitch with one strand of deep red thread; use two strands of yellow thread for the French knots.

4. When you have completed the embroidery, lightly press it on the wrong side with a steam iron. Mount the embroidery in the flexi-frame, making sure it is centred correctly (see page 12).

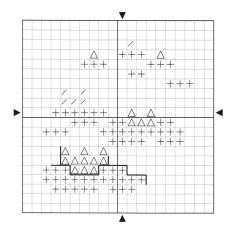

WATER-LILY GIFT TAG *(left)*, PICTURE & CARD *(right)*

		ANCHOR	DMC	MADEIRA
/	Pale peach	6	754	0404
△	Medium peach	10	352	0406
+	Medium green	266	471	1502
▬	Dark green	267	470	1503
	Deep red*	43	816	512
	Yellow**	289	307	0103

Backstitch outline
Flowers and leaves: One strand of deep red

**French knots*
● Flowers: Two strands of yellow

WATER-LILY CARD

Project time: TWO DAYS

Say it with flowers – this delicate hand-stitched card will show someone how much you care.

Skill level: BEGINNER

14-count pale blue Aida, 12.5 cm (5 in) square (you will need more fabric if you wish to work the design in a frame)

Tacking thread

Sewing needle

No 26 tapestry needle

One skein of stranded embroidery cotton (floss) in each of the colours given in the panel

Card with a 6 cm (2½ in) circular aperture

Solid glue stick

● These instructions are a quick-reference guide for this project. For more detailed information see Basic Techniques, page 8.

1. Mark the centre of the fabric with one vertical and one horizontal line of tacking (basting). This design can be worked either hand-held or placed in a frame.

2. Start the embroidery in the centre of the fabric and cross stitch the design, following the chart and using two strands of thread.

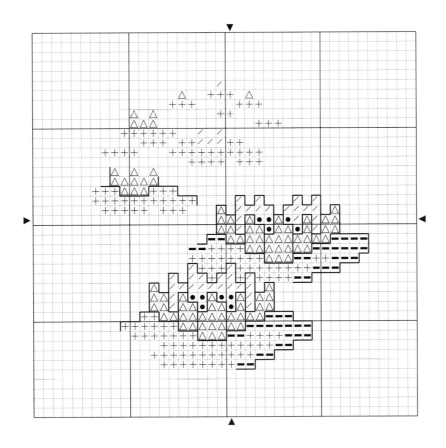

3. Outline the water-lily flowers and leaves in backstitch using one strand of deep red embroidery cotton (floss); use two strands of yellow embroidery cotton (floss) for the French knots.

4. When you have finished the embroidery, trim surplus material leaving a border of 12 mm (½ in) extra all round the design. Your work should measure 7.5 cm (3 in) square.

5. Open the card and spread glue evenly on the mounting flap (you can see this through the aperture when the card is closed). Place the embroidery in position and lightly press on the closed card to secure the embroidery.

IRIS SCISSORS' CASE

Project time: ONE WEEK

Start an iris needlecraft set with this scissors' case, adjusting it slightly, as necessary, to suit the size of your own scissors. It also makes a generous gift for a fellow craft lover.

Skill level: BEGINNER/IMPROVER

14-count pale blue Aida, 35.5 x 12.5 cm (14 x 5 in) – you will need more fabric if you wish to work your design in a frame

Tacking thread

Sewing needle

No 26 tapestry needle

Medium-weight iron-on interfacing, 30.5 x 10 cm (12 x 4 in)

One skein of stranded embroidery cotton (floss) in each of the colours given in the panel

Matching sewing thread

● These instructions are a quick-reference guide for this project. For more detailed information see Basic Techniques, page 8.

1. Fold the fabric in half lengthways and prepare to work the design on the top half of the fabric so that the fold will form the bottom of the case. Mark the centre of this section with one vertical and one horizontal line of tacking (basting). This design can be worked either hand-held or in a frame.

2. Start the embroidery in the centre of the prepared section and cross stitch the design, following the chart on page 42 and using two strands of embroidery cotton (floss).

3. Outline the flowers and stems in backstitch with one strand of dark green embroidery cotton (floss).

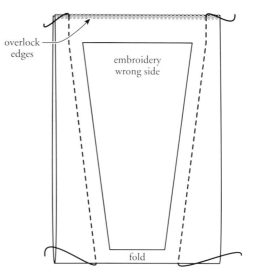

overlock edges

embroidery wrong side

fold

Stitching the seams

4. When you've completed the embroidery, trim surplus material. Your work should measure 30.5 x 10 cm (12 x 4in).

5. Fuse the interfacing to the wrong side of the fabric, then overlock the two short edges. Fold the fabric in half with right sides facing inwards.

Below The iris scissors' case and pin cushion are both one week projects

6. With the fabric fold at the bottom and right sides still facing inwards, machine a shaped seam starting approximately 12 mm (½ in) from each side edge of the embroidery (see diagram below left) – you may find it helpful to mark the stitching line with a pencil first. You may also wish to adjust the width of the side seams to the measurement of your scissors. Note that the machine stitching should straighten at the top of the case for 3 mm (1¼ in) to allow for the hem.

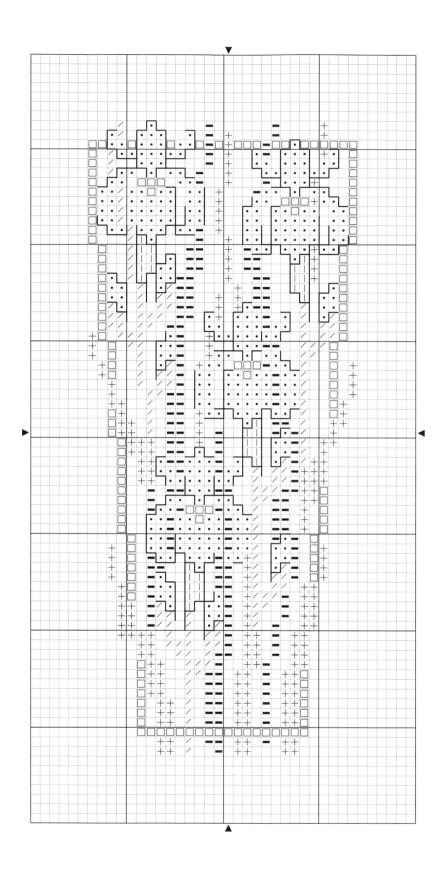

7. Trim surplus fabric from the sides leaving 6 mm (¼ in) seams, then overlock the raw edges.

8. Turn the fabric down at the opening to form a 1.5 cm (⅝ in) hem and slip stitch it.

9. Turn the work to the right side. Carefully use the end of a pencil to push out the base corners. If the fabric doesn't lie flat, trim the seam allowance at the bottom corners a little more for ease, taking care not to cut into the seam.

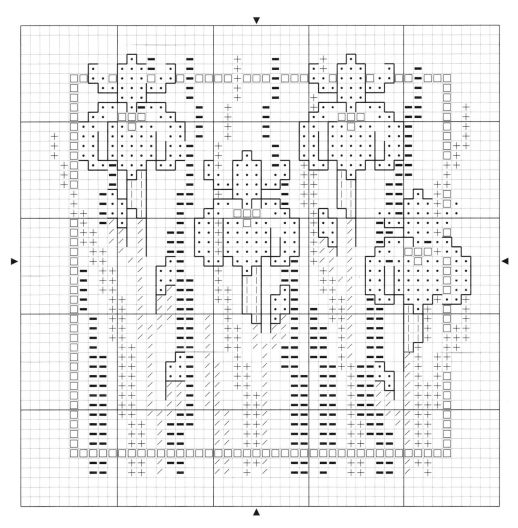

IRIS SCISSORS' CASE *(left)*
& PIN CUSHION *(above)*

		ANCHOR	DMC	MADEIRA
·	Yellow	289	307	0103
☐	Medium peach	10	352	0406
∣	Light green	265	3348	1501
╱	Medium green	266	471	1502
+	Dark green	267	470	1503
▬	Very dark green	268	469	1504

Backstitch outline
Flowers and stems: One strand of dark green

IRIS PIN CUSHION

Project time: ONE WEEK

Gorgeous yellow iris flowers explode out of the red border on this charming pin cushion.

Skill level: BEGINNER/IMPROVER

14-count pale blue Aida, 15.5 cm (6 in) square (you will need more fabric if you wish to work the design in a frame)

Tacking thread

Sewing needle

No 26 tapestry needle

One skein of stranded embroidery cotton (floss) in each of the colours given in the panel

12.5 cm (5 in) square of cotton backing fabric

Wadding (batting) for the cushion filling

Pale blue sewing thread

● These instructions are a quick-reference guide for this project. For more detailed information see Basic Techniques, page 8.

1. Mark the centre of the fabric with one vertical and one horizontal line of tacking (basting). This design can be worked either hand-held or placed in a frame.

2. Start the embroidery in the centre of the fabric and cross stitch the design, following the chart on page 43 and using two strands of embroidery cotton (floss).

3. Outline the flowers and stems in backstitch with one strand of dark green embroidery cotton (floss).

4. Trim surplus material leaving 2.5 cm (1 in) all round the design. Your work should measure 12.5 cm (5 in) square.

5. Place the embroidery and backing fabric together, right sides facing, and machine a seam round three sides, 12 mm (½ in) from the edges. Trim the allowances at corners.

6. Turn the work out and lightly press it, then fill it with small pieces of wadding (batting). When it is firm, turn in the open end and slip stitch it closed.

WATER GARDEN PICTURE *(opposite)*

		ANCHOR	DMC	MADEIRA
−	White	1	White	White
U	Yellow	289	307	0103
I	Pale peach	6	754	0404
V	Medium peach	10	352	0406
+	Pale plum	77	3687	0604
T	Brown	374	420	2104
·	Pale apple green	206	966	1210
/	Light green	265	3348	1501
X	Medium green	266	471	1502
O	Dark green	267	470	1503
▬	Very dark green	268	469	1504

Longstitch
Waterfall: Two strands of pale apple green
Iris leaves: Two strands of medium green

WATER GARDEN PICTURE

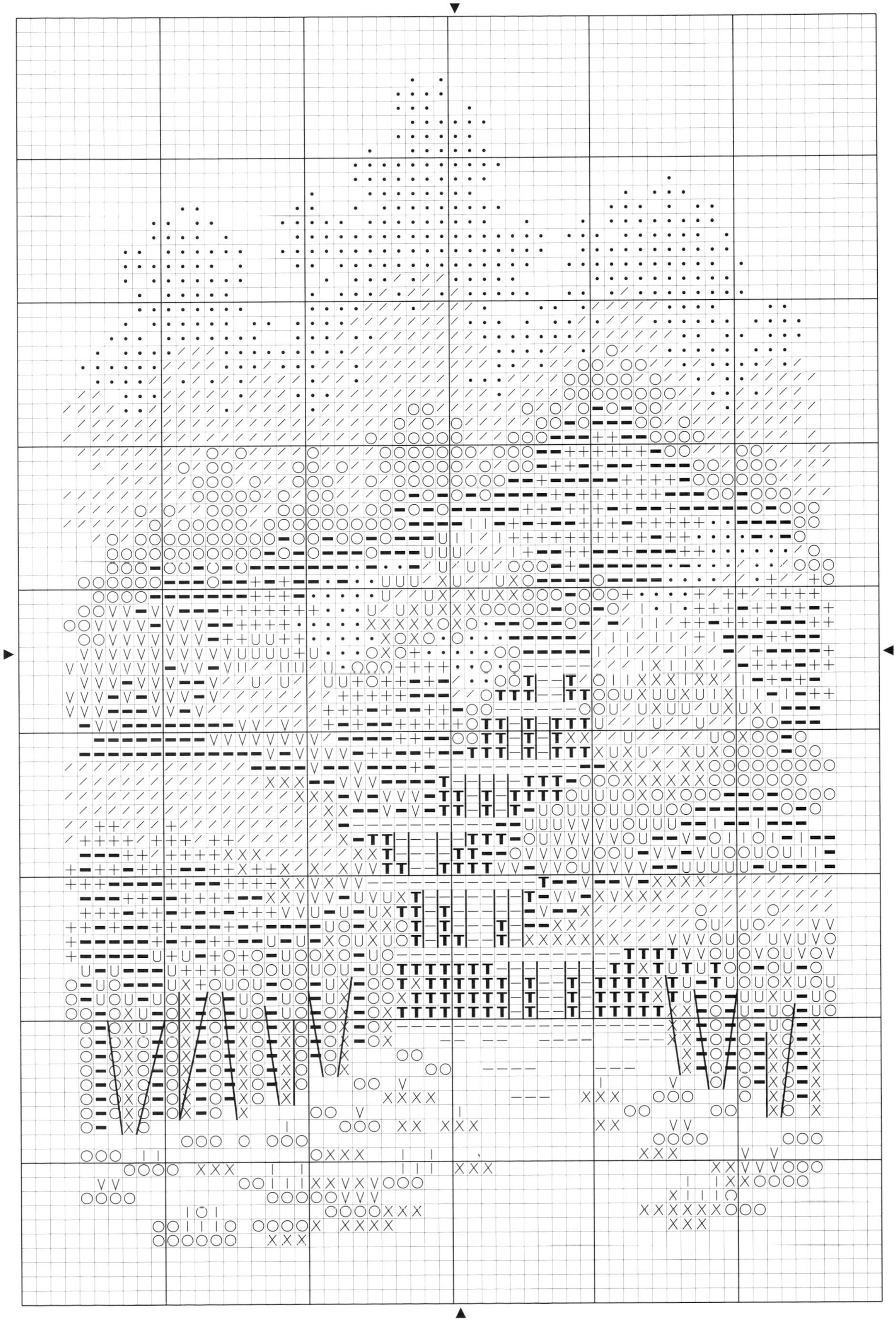

WATER GARDEN PICTURE

Project time: TWO WEEKS

Water tumbles into a tranquil pool where irises, water lilies and other water plants thrive. Bushes and shrubs reach upwards behind them, leading the eye into the distance.

Skill level: IMPROVER/EXPERIENCED

FOR THE EMBROIDERY

14-count pale blue Aida, 25.5 × 20 cm (10 × 8 in)

Tacking thread

Sewing needle

Embroidery frame

No 26 tapestry needle

One skein of stranded embroidery cotton (floss) in each of the colours given in the panel

FOR MOUNTING AND FRAMING

Frame with a 17.5 × 12.5 cm (7 × 5 in) internal aperture

Firm card, 17.5 × 12.5 cm (7 × 5 in)

Lightweight wadding (batting) 17.5 × 12.5 cm (7 × 5 in)

Solid glue stick

Strong thread for lacing

● These instructions are a quick-reference guide for this project. For more detailed information see Basic Techniques, page 8. For details on lacing see Basic Techniques, page 11.

1. Mark the centre of the fabric with one vertical and one horizontal line of tacking (basting). Place the prepared fabric in a suitable embroidery frame.

2. Start the embroidery in the centre of the fabric and cross stitch the design, following the chart and using two strands of thread.

3. Once the cross stitching is complete, longstitch the waterfall using two strands of pale apple green thread; use two strands of medium green thread to longstitch the slender iris leaves.

4. Remove the embroidery from the frame, handwash it if necessary (using a detergent suitable for delicates) and lightly press on the wrong side with a steam iron.

5. Spread glue evenly on one side of the card and lightly press the wadding (batting) down on top.

6. Centre the embroidery right side up over the padded card and secure it on the back with lacing.

7. Finally, assemble the frame following the manufacturer's instructions.

THE
*M*EDITERRANEAN
GARDEN

*The hot, spicy colours of Continental flowers are enlivened by the contrast of cool
stonework in a Mediterranean courtyard. To me, these colours always conjure
up pictures of cooking, so I have devoted this chapter to the kitchen, although you can
carry these designs into other areas of your home if you wish – the pomegranate
and nasturtium designs also make particularly attractive pictures for a conservatory.*

Pomegranate branches, laden with fruit,
Are warmed against the white-washed wall,
And in blazing Mediterranean heat,
Geranium buds are sun-flushed and full.

In the cool shadow of the garden gate
Lies the brightly coloured nasturtium bed.
These flowers burn bold in a distant land,
With flames of yellow and orange-tinged red.

GERANIUM GIFT TAG

Project time: TWO HOURS

A single bright red geranium flower ensures that this gift won't go unnoticed.

Skill level: BEGINNER

14-count cream Aida, 7.5 cm (3 in) square (you will need more fabric if you wish to work the design in a frame)

Tacking thread

Sewing needle

No 26 tapestry needle

One skein of stranded embroidery cotton (floss) in each of the colours given in the panel

Gift tag with a 3.5 cm (1³⁄₈ in) square aperture

Solid glue stick

● **These instructions are a quick-reference guide for this project. For more detailed information see Basic Techniques, page 8.**

1. Mark the centre of the fabric with tacking (basting). This design can be worked either hand-held or placed in a frame.

2. Start the embroidery in the centre of the fabric and cross stitch the design, following the chart on page 52 and using two strands of embroidery cotton (floss).

3. Backstitch the flower stalks using two strands of light green thread.

4. Trim surplus material leaving a 12 mm (½ in) border all round the design. The trimmed work should be about 2.5 cm (1 in) larger than the aperture on the tag.

5. Spread glue on the mounting flap (you can see this flap through the aperture when the card is closed). Place the embroidery in position and lightly press it to secure.

Opposite *The items in the geranium gift set can be worked together in a week*

GERANIUM REFRIGERATOR MAGNET

Project time: TWO DAYS

*Keep your shopping list handy by securing it to the front of the refrigerator with this embroidered magnet,
or adapt the idea to decorate a magnet with one of the other pretty designs in this book.*

Skill level: BEGINNER

14-count cream Aida, 12.5 cm (5 in) square (you
will need more fabric if you wish to work the
design in a frame)

Tacking thread

Sewing needle

No 26 tapestry needle

One skein of stranded embroidery cotton (floss)
in bright red and light green (see panel)

Medium-weight iron-on interfacing, 12.5 cm (5 in)
square

Refrigerator magnet, 7.5 x 5 cm (3 x 2 in)

● These instructions are a quick-reference guide
for this project. For more detailed information see
Basic Techniques, page 8.

1. Mark the centre of the fabric with one
vertical and one horizontal line of tacking

(basting). This design can be worked either
hand-held or placed in a frame.

2. Start the embroidery in the centre of the
fabric and cross stitch the design, following
the chart and using two strands of
embroidery cotton (floss).

3. Outline the pot and leaves in backstitch,
using one strand of dark red thread.
Backstitch the flower stalks with two strands
of light green thread.

4. Place the iron-on interfacing, glue side
down, on the back of the work and bond by
lightly ironing.

5. Trim the fabric to the size of the magnet
case and assemble following the
manufacturer's instructions.

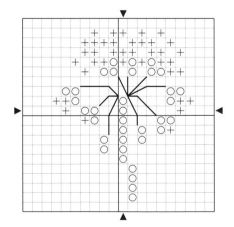

GERANIUM GIFT TAG *(left)*, CARD & REFRIGERATOR MAGNET *(right)*

		ANCHOR	DMC	MADEIRA
+	Bright red	46	666	0210
○	Light green	256	906	1411
−	Beige	372	738	2013
·	Pale yellow-green	253	772	1409
▬	Medium green	258	904	1413
X	Dark red	20	498	0513
/	Light terracotta	338	921	0402
■	Dark terracotta	339	920	0401

Backstitch outline
Flower stalks: Two strands of light green
Pot and leaves: One strand of dark red

GERANIUM GREETINGS CARD

Project time: TWO DAYS

Bright red geraniums are a cheerful sight on balconies and in gardens everywhere. These make a greetings card that will lighten the spirits.

Skill level: BEGINNER

14-count cream Aida, 12.5 cm (5 in) square (you will need more fabric if you wish to work the design in a frame)

Tacking thread

Sewing needle

No 26 tapestry needle

One skein of stranded embroidery cotton (floss) in each of the colours given in the panel

Card with a 7.5 x 5.5 cm (3 x 2¼ in) aperture

Solid glue stick

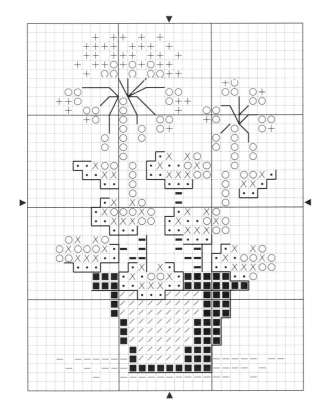

● These instructions are a quick-reference guide for this project. For more detailed information see Basic Techniques, page 8.

1. Mark the centre of the fabric with one vertical and one horizontal line of tacking (basting). This design can be worked either hand-held or placed in a frame.

2. Start the embroidery in the centre of the fabric and cross stitch the design, following the chart and using two strands of thread.

3. Outline the pot and leaves in backstitch using one strand of dark red thread. Backstitch the flower stalks with two strands of light green thread.

4. When you have finished the embroidery, trim surplus material leaving a 12 mm (½ in) border all round the design. Your work should measure 10 x 7.5 cm (4 x 3 in).

5. Open the card and spread glue evenly on the mounting flap (you can see this through the aperture when the card is closed). Place the embroidery in position and lightly press on the closed card to secure.

COLOURFUL POT COVERS

Project time: ONE WEEK

Brightly coloured nasturtiums and exotic pomegranates make the perfect motifs for a pair of cheering pot covers. Use one on a jar of delicious home-made jam and the other on your favourite marmalade. Trim with bright matching ribbon.

Skill level: BEGINNER

7.5 cm (3 in) 18-count cream Aida circular pot cover for each design

Tacking thread

Sewing needle

No 26 tapestry needle

One skein of stranded embroidery cotton (floss) in each of the colours given in the panel

12mm (½ in) wide ribbon, 50cm (20 in) long for each design

● These instructions are a quick-reference guide for this project. For more detailed information see Basic Techniques, page 8.

1. Mark the centre of the fabric with one vertical and one horizontal line of tacking (basting). Each design can be worked either hand-held or placed in a frame.

NASTURTIUM POT COVER *(below)*

		ANCHOR	DMC	MADEIRA
+	Yellow	306	783	0114
·	Pale yellow-green	253	772	1409
↓	Light green	256	906	1411
◹	Medium green	258	904	1413
○	Bright red	46	666	0210
●	Medium red	19	321	0511
	Dark red*	20	498	0513

Backstitch outline
Flowers and leaves: One strand of dark red

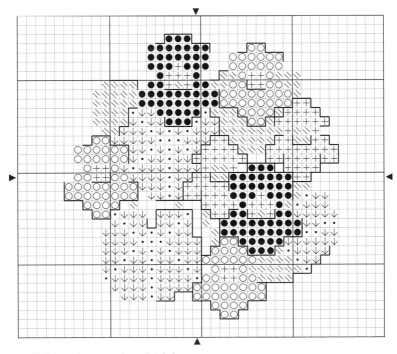

Opposite *Pomegranate (left) and nasturtium (right) pot covers*

2. Start the embroidery in the centre of the fabric and cross stitch the design, following the chart and using one strand of thread.

3. Outline the flowers and fruit or leaves in backstitch as indicated in the appropriate chart, using one strand of dark red embroidery cotton (floss).

4. Finally, thread the ribbon through the eyelets on the lace border and tie the ends together in a neat bow.

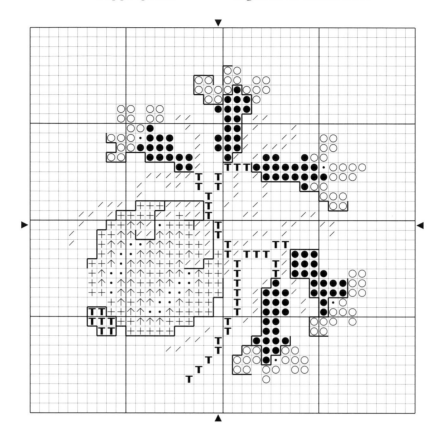

POMEGRANATE POT COVER *(above)*

		ANCHOR	DMC	MADEIRA
·	Yellow	306	783	0114
↑	Light terracotta	338	921	0402
+	Dark terracotta	339	920	0401
T	Brown	359	898	2006
/	Light green	256	906	1411
○	Bright red	46	666	0210
●	Medium red	19	321	0511
	Dark red*	20	498	0513

Backstitch outline
Pomegranate and flowers: One strand of dark red

MEDITERRANEAN GARDEN PICTURE *(right)*

		ANCHOR	DMC	MADEIRA
I	Cream	386	712	2014
+	Beige	372	738	2013
V	Yellow	306	783	0114
U	Light terracotta	338	921	0402
T	Brown	359	898	2006
○	Bright red	46	666	0210
●	Medium red	19	321	0511
X	Dark red	20	498	0513
·	Pale yellow-green	253	772	1409
/	Light green	256	906	1411
╲	Medium green	258	904	1413
■	Dark green	879	500	1705

Backstitch outline
Bricks, fruit, pots and leaves: One strand of dark green

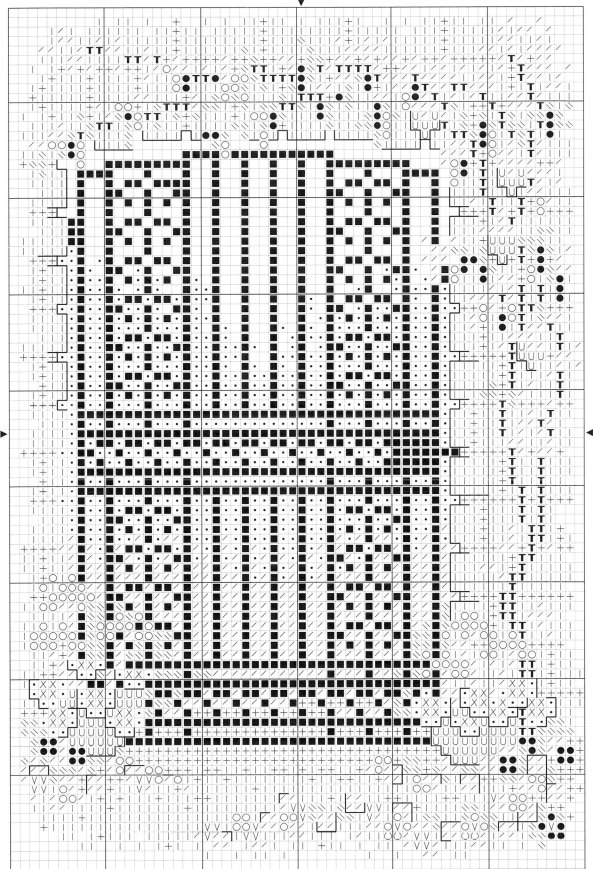

MEDITERRANEAN GARDEN PICTURE

Project time: TWO WEEKS

Gates are always an appealing subject for a picture because it's intriguing to know where they lead to – or from. Judging by the thriving plants here, this gate belongs somewhere really special.

Skill level: IMPROVER/EXPERIENCED

FOR THE EMBROIDERY

14-count cream Aida, 25.5 x 20 cm (10 x 8 in)

Tacking thread

Sewing needle

Embroidery frame

No 26 tapestry needle

One skein of stranded embroidery cotton (floss) in each of the colours given in the panel

FOR MOUNTING AND FRAMING

Frame with a 17.5 x 12.5 cm (7 x 5 in) internal aperture

Firm card, 17.5 x 12.5 cm (7 x 5 in)

Lightweight wadding (batting), 17.5 x 12.5 cm (7 x 5 in)

Solid glue stick

Strong thread for lacing

● These instructions are a quick-reference guide for this project. For more detailed information see Basic Techniques, page 8. For information on lacing see Basic Techniques, page 11.

1. Mark the centre of the fabric with one vertical and one horizontal line of tacking (basting). Place the fabric in a frame.

2. Start the embroidery in the centre of the fabric and cross stitch the design, following the chart on page 57 and using two strands of embroidery cotton (floss).

3. Outline the embroidery in backstitch using one strand of dark green thread.

4. Remove the embroidery from the frame, wash it, if necessary, and lightly press with a steam iron on the wrong side.

5. Spread glue evenly on one side of the firm card and lightly press the wadding (batting) on top.

6. Centre the embroidery over the padded card and secure it with lacing.

7. Finally, assemble the frame following the manufacturer's instructions.

THE
WILD FLOWER
GARDEN

*Wild flowers are becoming increasingly popular, and it's not
uncommon to find them mixed with herbaceous plants in many
borders. All the flowers in this chapter grow in my own garden, so it
gave me great pleasure to include them in the design for the book cover
and bookmark. Many of the designs are adaptable – the bookmark
could be repeated to make a cake band, and the coaster design would
make a pretty top for a trinket box.*

In the field, amongst the trees,
Wild flowers scent the breeze.
There the scarlet pimpernel,
Blushing, hides with blue speedwell.

Above the grasses, dandelions bright
Bloom by poppies in quiet delight.
There sweet violets nod their heads,
Ambling round the periwinkle beds.

Yellow loosestrife joins the dance,
And in the wind these flowers prance.
And now no more may this poet tell,
Of the wildflower garden by the wishing well.

PERIWINKLE GIFT TAG

Project time: TWO HOURS

Tiny scarlet pimpernel flowers swirl around a lovely blue periwinkle on this colourful gift tag. The yellow card echoes the bright centre of the periwinkle, completing the vivid effect.

SKILL LEVEL: BEGINNER

14-count white Aida, 7.5 cm (3 in) square (allow more if you wish to work the design in a frame)

Tacking thread

Sewing needle

No 26 tapestry needle

One skein of stranded embroidery cotton (floss) in each of the colours shown in the chart

Gift tag with a 3.5 cm (1⅜ in) square aperture

Solid glue stick

● These instructions are a quick-reference guide for this project. For more detailed information see Basic Techniques, page 8.

1. Mark the centre of the fabric with one vertical and one horizontal line of tacking (basting). This design can be worked either hand-held or placed in a frame.

2. Start the embroidery in the centre of the fabric and cross stitch the design, following the chart on page 64 and using two strands of embroidery cotton (floss).

3. Outline the blue periwinkle in backstitch using one strand of dark blue thread.

Opposite *The periwinkle gift set can be completed in less than a week*

4. When you have finished the embroidery, trim surplus material leaving a 12 mm (½ in) border all round the design. The trimmed work should be approximately 2.5 cm (1 in) larger than the aperture.

5. Spread glue evenly on the mounting flap (you can see this through the aperture when the card is closed). Carefully place the embroidery in position and lightly press to secure it in the card.

PERIWINKLE COASTER

Project time: TWO DAYS

The tiny red flowers of the scarlet pimpernel close in bad weather, but on this coaster, with its ring of bright yellow card, it will always be a sunny day.

Skill level: BEGINNER/IMPROVER

14-count white Aida, 12.5 cm (5 in) square (you will need more fabric if you wish to work the design in a frame)

Tacking thread

Sewing needle

No 26 tapestry needle

One skein of stranded embroidery cotton (floss) in each of the colours shown in the chart

Medium-weight iron-on interfacing, 12.5 cm (5 in) square

Coaster with a 7.5 cm (3 in) circular aperture

Piece of card larger than the coaster for the mount (optional)

● These instructions are a quick-reference guide for this project. For more detailed information see Basic Techniques, page 8.

1. Mark the centre of the fabric with one vertical and one horizontal line of tacking (basting). This design can be worked either hand-held or placed in a frame.

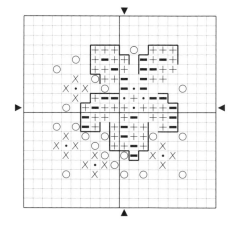

2. Start the embroidery in the centre of the fabric and cross stitch the design, following the chart opposite and using two strands of embroidery cotton (floss).

3. Outline the blue periwinkle in backstitch using one strand of dark blue thread.

4. Place the interfacing glue-side down on the back of the work and bond by lightly ironing.

5. Trim the fabric to the size of the coaster using the coaster's plastic backing disc as a template – make sure the work is properly centred before cutting.

6. The mount is optional and was made from a card with a 6 cm (2½ in) circular aperture. Again you can use the backing disc as a template to mark a cutting line.

7. Finally, assemble the coaster following the manufacturer's instructions.

PERIWINKLE GIFT TAG *(left)*, **COASTER** *(above right)* & **CARD** *(below right)*

		ANCHOR	DMC	MADEIRA
·	Yellow	290	973	0105
X	Red	29	891	0411
O	Light green	225	703	1307
+	Light blue	140	809	0909
−	Medium blue	146	798	1004
V	Golden yellow	298	972	0107
I	Medium green	227	701	1305
	Dark blue*	162	825	1011

Backstitch outline
Periwinkles: One strand of dark blue

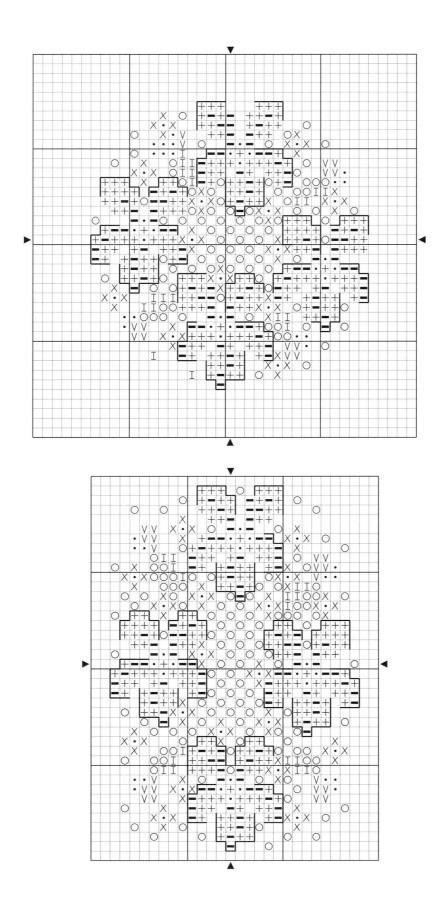

PERIWINKLE GREETINGS CARD

Project time: TWO DAYS

An oval of red, yellow and blue wild flowers graces the front of this bright greetings card, the final piece in the periwinkle gift set.

Skill level: BEGINNER/IMPROVER

14-count white Aida, 12.5 cm (5 in) square (you will need more fabric if you wish to work the design in a frame)

Tacking thread

Sewing needle

No 26 tapestry needle

One skein of stranded embroidery cotton (floss) in each of the colours given in the panel

Card with a 7.5 x 5.5 cm (3 x 2¼ in) aperture

Solid glue stick

● These instructions are a quick-reference guide for this project. For more detailed information see Basic Techniques, page 8.

1. Mark the centre of the fabric with one vertical and one horizontal line of tacking (basting). This design can be worked either hand-held or placed in a frame.

2. Start the embroidery in the centre of the fabric and cross stitch the design, following the chart and using two strands of thread.

3. Outline the blue periwinkle in backstitch using one strand of dark blue thread.

4. When you have finished the embroidery, trim surplus material leaving a 12 mm (½ in) border all round the design. Your work should measure 10 x 7.5 cm (4 x 3 in).

5. Open the card and spread glue evenly on the mounting flap (you can see this through the aperture when the card is closed). Place the embroidery in position and lightly press the closed card to secure.

WILD FLOWER BOOK COVER

Project time: ONE WEEK

A merry mix of dandelions, violets, scarlet pimpernel, periwinkle and speedwell scamper down a book cover that's perfect for a diary or your favourite gardening book.

Skill level: EXPERIENCED

FOR THE EMBROIDERY

14-count white Aida, 28 × 15 cm (11 × 6 in) – allow more material to work the design in your frame

Embroidery frame

Tacking thread

Sewing needle

No 26 tapestry needle

One skein of stranded embroidery cotton (floss) in each of the colours given in the panel

FOR THE BOOK COVER

Medium-weight blue cotton, 42 × 25.5 cm (16½ × 10 in)

Medium-weight iron-on interfacing, 42 × 25.5 cm (16½ × 10 in)

Matching sewing cotton

Sharp needle

1. Mark the centre of the fabric with one vertical and one horizontal line of tacking (basting). Place the fabric in a frame.

2. Start the embroidery in the centre of the fabric and cross stitch the design, following the chart and using two strands of thread. Continue the repeat pattern until the embroidered panel measures 20 cm (8 in).

3. Outline the blue periwinkles in backstitch with one strand of dark blue thread; outline the violets with one strand of dark lilac. Work French knots for the dandelion centres in two strands of yellow.

4. Cut away surplus material leaving 2 cm (¾ in) on each side of the embroidery and 2.5 cm (1 in) at the top and bottom.

• The instructions are for a 20 × 14 cm (8 × 5½ in) book with a 12 mm (½ in) spine. For a customized cover, measure the book, including the width of the spine, and add 12.5 cm (5 in) to the width for the flaps and 5 cm (2 in) to the length for top and bottom turnings. You may find it helpful to create a paper pattern and try it for fit first. Adjust the cross-stitch design to fit.

• These instructions are a quick-reference guide for this project. For more detailed information see Basic Techniques, page 8.

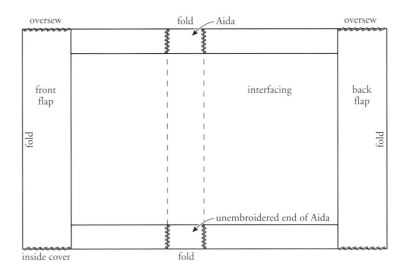

Constructing the book cover

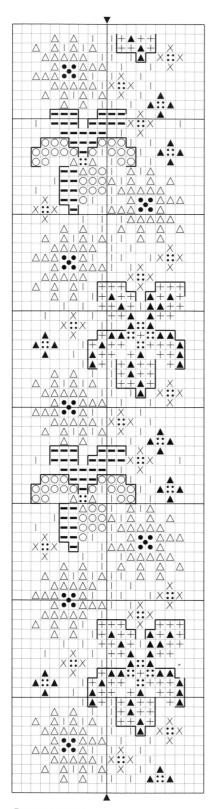

Repeat pattern

WILD FLOWER BOOK COVER & BOOKMARK

		ANCHOR	DMC	MADEIRA
::	Yellow	290	973	0105
△	Golden yellow	298	972	0107
X	Red	29	891	0411
O	Light lilac	109	209	0803
−	Medium lilac	110	208	0804
I	Light green	225	703	1307
+	Light blue	140	809	0909
▲	Medium blue	146	798	1004
	Dark blue*	162	825	1011
	Dark lilac*	111	327	0714

Backstitch outline
Periwinkles: One strand of dark blue
Violets: One strand of dark lilac

French knots
●   Dandelion centres: Two strands of yellow

5. Fold the fabric at the sides of the embroidery to the back of the work, leaving a small white border on each side. Lightly press on the back of the work with a steam iron.

6. Place the interfacing, glue-side down, on the back of the cover fabric and fuse in place by ironing. Fold back a 2.5 cm (1 in) turning at the top of the fabric and press with a steam iron. Repeat at the bottom of the fabric.

7. Turn a 12 mm (½ in) hem at each side of the cover and slip stitch in place. Fold the fabric again to create a 5 cm (2 in) flap at each end and attach to the back of the cover by oversewing at the top and bottom edges.

8. Fit the cover on the book and place the embroidery in the desired position with a 2.5 cm (1 in) fabric allowance at the top and bottom. Pin the work to the cover and remove the cover from the book.

9. Secure the band to the cover by slip stitching neatly along each side of the embroidery. Finally, turn the top and bottom flaps to the wrong side of the work and slip stitch in place to secure.

WILD FLOWER BOOKMARK

Project time: ONE WEEK

Keep your place in this book using the pretty hand-stitched bookmark shown here, or use it with the matching wild flower book cover. It also makes a very generous present, particularly with the gift of a book.

Skill level: IMPROVER

14-count white Aida, 28 × 15 cm (11 × 6 in) – allow extra fabric to work the design in your frame

Embroidery frame

Tacking thread

Sewing needle

No 26 tapestry needle

One skein of stranded embroidery cotton (floss) in each of the colours given in the panel

White sewing cotton

● The bookmark is 23 × 4 cm (9 × 1½ in). However, the design is based on a repeat pattern and you can lengthen or shorten it to suit your own particular requirements.
● These instructions are a quick-reference guide for this project. For more detailed information see Basic Techniques, page 8.

Below The book cover and matching bookmark are ideal for book lovers everywhere, and each one will take only a week to stitch

1. Mark the centre of the fabric with one vertical and one horizontal line of tacking (basting). Place the prepared fabric in an embroidery frame.

2. Start the embroidery in the centre of the fabric and cross stitch the design, following the chart on page 68 and using two strands of thread. Continue the pattern until the panel measures 19 cm (7½ in).

3. Outline the blue periwinkles in backstitch with one strand of dark blue thread; to backstitch the violets use one strand of dark lilac thread. Work French knots for the dandelion centres with two strands of yellow thread.

4. Cut away surplus material so the fabric measures 23 x 9 cm (9 x 3½ in) with the embroidery in the centre of the trimmed area. Run a single line of cross stitching immediately above and just below the embroidered panel using ordinary white sewing cotton.

5. Tease out the threads at each end of the bookmark to create the fringed edging. The fringe can be trimmed on completion of the bookmark to straighten the edges.

6. Fold the fabric on each side of the embroidery to the back of the work, leaving a small white border on each edge to frame the design. Lightly press the turnings with a steam iron on the back of the work, using a pressing cloth to protect it.

7. Fold in one of the flaps to make a 6 mm (¼ in) hem and attach to the other flap by neatly slip stitching down the complete length of the bookmark.

WILD FLOWER GARDEN PICTURE

Project time: TWO WEEKS

Poppies and dandelions dance in the breeze, while periwinkles twine through the picket fence and speedwell and tiny scarlet pimpernel seek the protection of the magical wishing well in this enchanting picture. Make your own wish while you stitch.

Skill level: IMPROVER/EXPERIENCED

FOR THE EMBROIDERY

14-count white Aida, 25.5 x 20 cm (10 x 8 in)

Tacking thread

Sewing needle

No 26 tapestry needle

One skein of stranded embroidery cotton (floss) in each of the colours given in the panel

Embroidery frame

FOR MOUNTING AND FRAMING

Frame with a 17.5 x 12.5 cm (7 x 5 in) internal aperture

Firm card, 17.5 x 12.5 cm (7 x 5 in)

Lightweight wadding (batting), 17.5 x 12.5 cm (7 x 5 in)

Solid glue stick

Strong thread for lacing

Opposite *The finished wild flower garden picture*

● These instructions are a quick-reference guide for this project. For more detailed information see Basic Techniques, page 8. For specific instructions on lacing see page 11.

1. Mark the centre of the fabric with one vertical and one horizontal line of tacking (basting). Place the prepared fabric in an embroidery frame.

2. Start the embroidery in the centre of the fabric and cross stitch the design, following the chart opposite and using two strands of embroidery cotton (floss).

3. Outline the embroidery in backstitch, using two strands of dark green thread for the well and birds. Stitch each bird individually and avoid taking dark threads from one bird to another because they may show through the back of the embroidery.

4. Satin stitch the well rope with all six strands of dark green thread, extending the final stitch down to the wall of the well. (For details on working satin stitch see Basic Techniques, page 10.)

5. Remove the embroidery from the frame, hand wash it, if necessary (using a detergent suitable for delicates), and lightly press it with a steam iron on the wrong side.

6. Spread glue evenly on one side of the firm card and lightly press the wadding (batting) on top.

7. Centre the embroidery over the padded card and secure with lacing.

8. Finally, assemble the frame following the manufacturer's instructions.

WILD FLOWER PICTURE *(right)*

		ANCHOR	DMC	MADEIRA
◇	Golden yellow	298	972	0107
■	Red	29	891	0411
I	Light blue	140	809	0909
+	Medium blue	146	798	1004
V	Violet	110	208	0804
·	Pale green	240	955	1209
\	Light green	225	703	1307
U	Medium green	227	701	1305
▬	Dark green	246	319	1405
─	Very light brown	347	436	0310
→	Light brown	374	420	2011
X	Medium brown	375	869	2302
○	Warm brown	349	301	2105
●	Dark brown	906	938	2114

Backstitch outline
Wishing well: Two strands of dark green
Birds: Two strands of dark green

Satin stitch
Well rope: Six strands of dark green

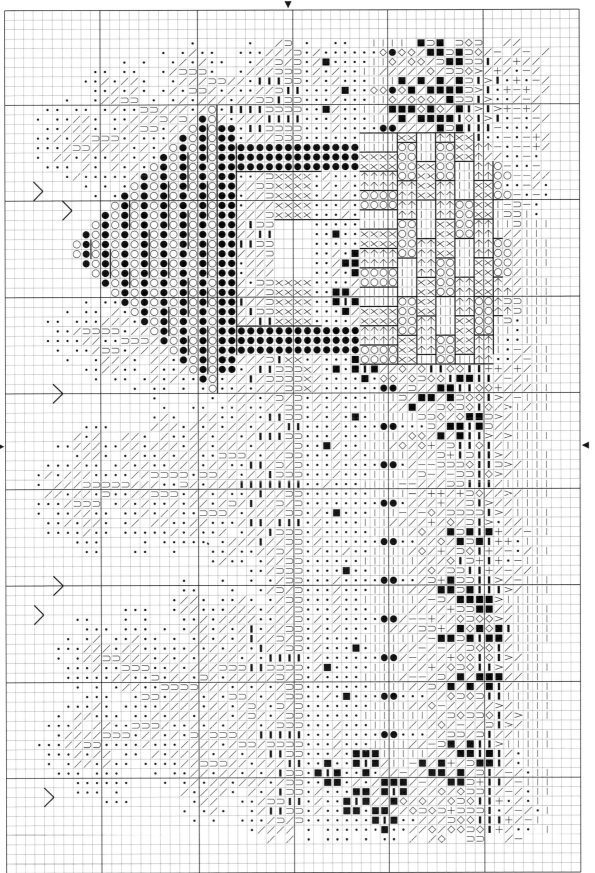

THE
JAPANESE
GARDEN

A Japanese garden, with its fascinating mixture of water, ornament and plant texture, is a wonderful subject for an embroidery, and I have tried to include all these features in my garden picture. Japanese gardens are often very colourful, so I have chosen a red and gold theme in this chapter. The rich colour combination adds brilliance to the co-ordinated gift set, and the golden lilies would enliven any room.

Built many years ago, the temple stands,
Encircled by a mist of acer trees.
This is a place to meditate in peace
Where gold Azaleas flutter in the breeze.

An ornamental bridge spans the river
Where lilies grow in beauty and in grace.
And here the storeys of the antique temple
Reflect back from the water's silvery face.

AZALEA GIFT TAG

Project time: TWO HOURS

This beautifully designed azalea flower captures the full loveliness of the real thing. It can be stitched in two hours, but it could last a lifetime.

Skill level: BEGINNER

14-count white Aida, 7.5 cm (3 in) square (you will need more fabric if you wish to work the design in a frame)

Tacking thread

Sewing needle

No 26 tapestry needle

One skein of stranded embroidery cotton (floss) in each of the colours given in the panel

Gift tag with a 3.5 cm (1⅜ in) circular or square aperture

Solid glue stick

● These instructions are a quick-reference guide for this project. For more detailed information see Basic Techniques, page 8.

1. Mark the centre of the fabric with one vertical and one horizontal line of tacking (basting). This design can be worked either hand-held or placed in a frame.

2. Start the embroidery in the centre of the fabric and cross stitch the design, following the chart and using two strands of thread.

3. When you have finished all the cross stitch, outline the flower in backstitch using one strand of brown thread; use the same colour to longstitch the stamens.

4. Trim surplus material leaving a 12 mm (½ in) border all round the embroidered design. The trimmed work should be approximately 2.5 cm (1 in) larger than the aperture on the gift tag.

5. Spread glue evenly on the mounting flap (you can see this through the aperture when the card is closed). Place the embroidery in position and lightly press the closed card to secure. Allow the glue to dry completely before you use the gift tag.

AZALEA TRINKET BOX

Project time: TWO HOURS

By working the design for the azalea gift tag on a fabric with a higher count, you can create a smaller version to frame in the lid of a trinket box.

Skill level: BEGINNER/IMPROVER

18-count white Aida, 7.5 cm (3 in) square (you will need more fabric if you wish to work the design in a frame)

Tacking thread

Sewing needle

No 26 tapestry needle

One skein of stranded embroidery cotton (floss) in each of the colours given in the panel

Trinket box with a 3 cm (1¼ in) circular aperture

Solid glue stick

● These instructions are a quick-reference guide for this project. For more detailed information see Basic Techniques, page 8.

1. Mark the centre of the fabric with one vertical and one horizontal line of tacking (basting). This design can be worked either hand-held or placed in a frame.

2. Start the embroidery in the centre of the fabric and cross stitch the design, following the chart and using one strand of thread.

3. When you have finished all the cross stitch, outline the flower in backstitch using one strand of brown thread; use the same colour to longstitch the stamens.

4. Trim surplus material so that the embroidery fits comfortably in the trinket box lid and assemble it following the manufacturer's instructions.

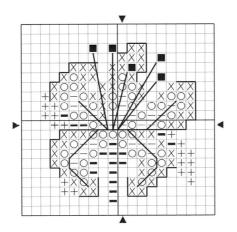

AZALEA GIFT TAG & TRINKET BOX *(left)*

		ANCHOR	DMC	MADEIRA
−	Pale yellow	293	727	0110
○	Medium yellow	305	743	0113
X	Golden yellow	298	972	0107
■	Brown	308	782	2302
+	Light green	238	703	1307
−	Medium green	258	904	1413

Backstitch outline
Flower: One strand of brown

Longstitch
Stamens: One strand of brown

AZALEA GREETINGS CARD

Project time: TWO DAYS

A ring of golden azalea flowers with their leaves entwined adorns this greetings card. Created from the motif used on the gift tag and trinket box, it completes the Japanese garden gift set.

14-count white Aida, 12.5 cm (5 in) square (you will need more fabric if you wish to work the design in a frame)

Tacking thread

Sewing needle

No 26 tapestry needle

One skein of stranded embroidery cotton (floss) in each of the colours given in the panel

Card with an 8 cm (3¼ in) circular aperture

Solid glue stick

• These instructions are a quick-reference guide for this project. For more detailed information see Basic Techniques, page 8.

1. Mark the centre of the fabric with one vertical and one horizontal line of tacking (basting). This design can be worked either hand-held or placed in a frame.

AZALEA GREETINGS CARD *(below)*

		ANCHOR	DMC	MADEIRA
−	Pale yellow	293	727	0110
○	Medium yellow	305	743	0113
×	Golden yellow	298	972	0107
■	Brown	308	782	2302
+	Light green	238	703	1307
▬	Medium green	258	904	1413

Backstitch outline
Flowers: One strand of brown

Longstitch
Stamens: One strand of brown

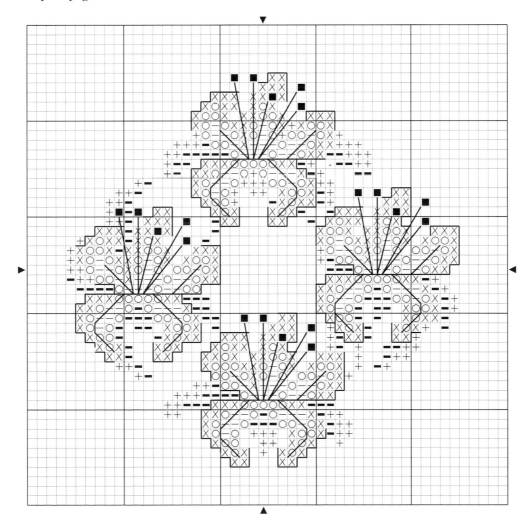

2. Start the embroidery in the centre of the fabric and cross stitch the design, following the chart on page 79 and using two strands of embroidery cotton (floss).

3. When you have finished all the cross stitch, complete the embroidery by adding the details: outline the flowers in backstitch using one strand of brown thread; use the same colour to longstitch the stamens.

4. On completion, trim surplus material leaving a 12 mm (½ in) border all round the design. Your work should now measure 10 cm (4 in) square.

5. Open the card and spread glue evenly on the mounting flap (you can see this flap through the aperture when the card is closed). Place the embroidery in position and lightly press on the closed card to secure.

GOLDEN LILIES HANGING

Project time: ONE WEEK

Glorious golden lilies burst into bloom on this pretty hanging. Make it longer if you wish, simply by repeating the pattern as often as you like.

Skill level: IMPROVER

14-count white Aida, 25.5 x 12.5 cm (10 x 5 in) – you will need more fabric to work the design in a frame

Tacking thread

Sewing needle

Embroidery frame

No 26 tapestry needle

One skein of stranded embroidery cotton (floss) in each of the colours given in the panel

White cotton backing, 25.5 x 10 cm (10 x 4 in)

White sewing cotton

Bell pull ends, 9 cm (3½ in) wide

● These instructions are a quick-reference guide for this project. For more detailed information see Basic Techniques, page 8.

1. Mark the centre of the fabric with one vertical and one horizontal line of tacking (basting). Place the prepared fabric in an embroidery frame.

2. Start the embroidery in the centre of the fabric and cross stitch the design, following the chart on page 82 and using two strands of embroidery cotton (floss).

3. Outline the flowers in backstitch using one strand of brown thread; work the stamens in longstitch using two strands of brown.

4. Remove the embroidery from the frame, wash if necessary, and lightly press on the wrong side with a steam iron.

5. Trim surplus fabric from the sides so that the embroidery measures 25.5 x 10 cm (10 x 4 in). Place the embroidery and backing fabric together, right sides facing, and machine stitch 6 mm (¼ in) side seams.

6. Turn the work to the right side and lightly press with a steam iron. Overlock the two ends to prevent fraying and assemble the bell pull following the manufacturer's instruction.

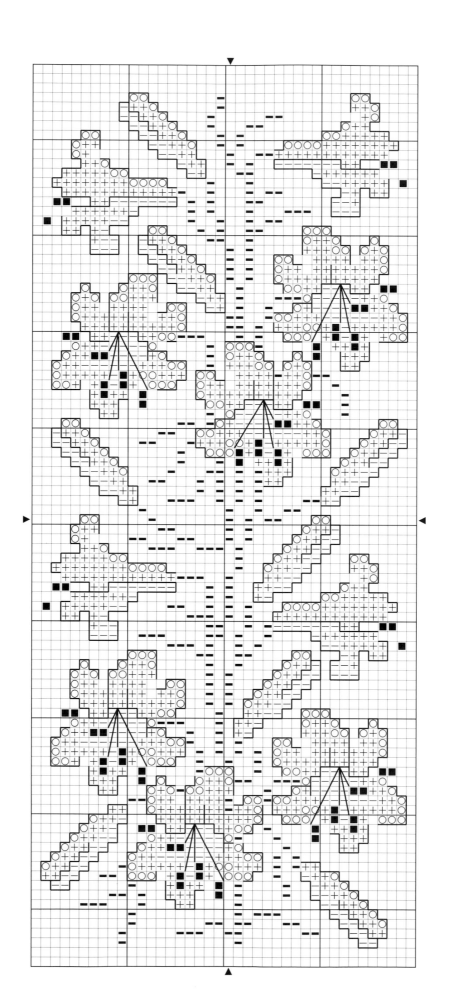

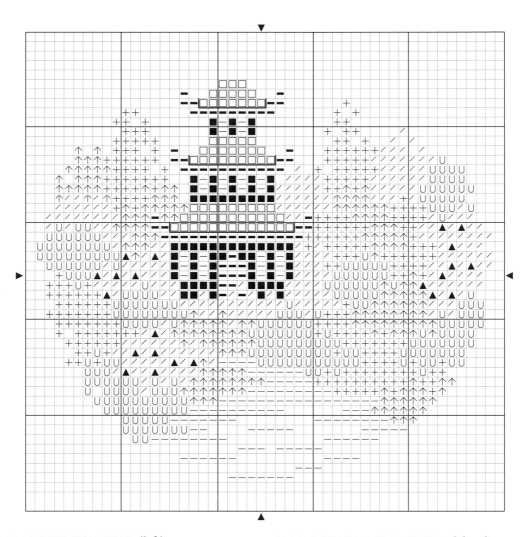

GOLDEN LILIES HANGING *(left)*

		ANCHOR	DMC	MADEIRA
○	Medium yellow	305	743	0113
+	Golden yellow	298	972	0107
−	Orange	303	742	0114
■	Brown	308	782	2302
▬	Green	238	703	1307

Backstitch outline
Lilies: One strand of brown

Longstitch
Stamens: Two strands of brown

JAPANESE TEMPLE PICTURE *(above)*

		ANCHOR	DMC	MADEIRA
−	Silver	847	3072	1709
▲	Medium yellow	305	743	0113
☐	Golden yellow	298	972	0107
▬	Orange	303	742	0114
■	Red	29	891	0411
U	Yellow-brown	308	782	2302
↑	Brown	355	975	2303
╱	Light green	238	703	1307
+	Medium green	258	904	1413

Backstitch outline
Temple roofs: One strand of red

TEMPLE PICTURE

Project time: ONE WEEK

Shown on the left, this is the first of two pictures featuring the exotic Japanese temple.

Skill level: IMPROVER

14-count white Aida, 20cm (8in) square

Tacking thread

Sewing needle

Embroidery frame

No 26 tapestry needle

One skein of stranded embroidery cotton (floss) in each of the colours given in the panel

White felt for backing, 12.5cm (5in) square

Flexi-frame, 10cm (4in) square

White sewing cotton

Strong thread for lacing

● **These instructions are a quick-reference guide for this project. For more detailed information see Basic Techniques, page 8.**

1. Mark the centre of the fabric with one vertical and one horizontal line of tacking (basting). Place the fabric in a frame.

2. Start the embroidery in the centre of the fabric and cross stitch the design, following the chart on page 83 and using two strands of embroidery cotton (floss).

3. Outline the temple roofs in backstitch using one strand of red thread.

4. Remove the embroidery from the frame, wash if necessary, and lightly press on the wrong side with a steam iron.

5. Mount the embroidery in the flexi-frame, following the manufacturer's instructions.

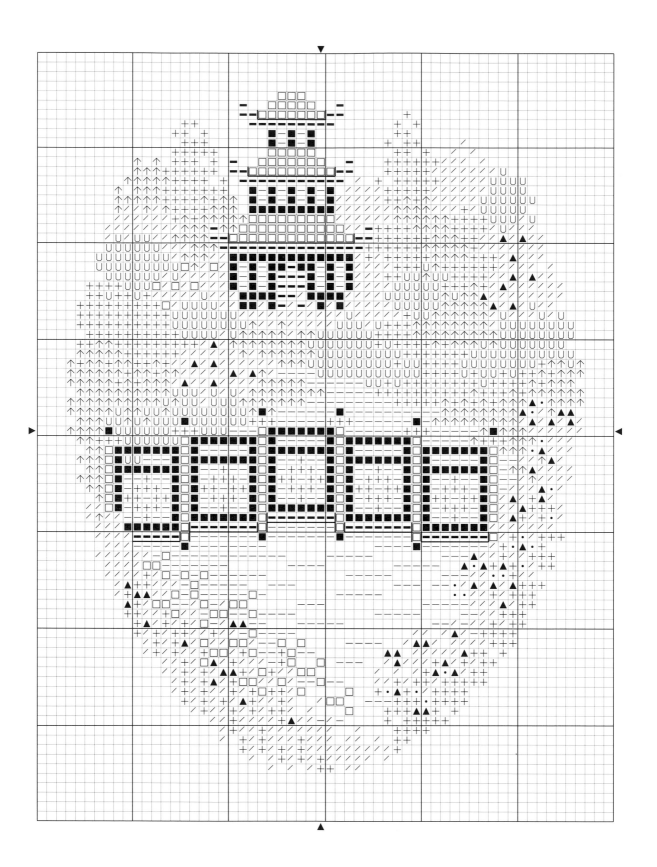

THE JAPANESE GARDEN PICTURE

Project time: TWO WEEKS

Rising out of a forest of reds, browns and greens, the Japanese temple dominates the treeline, while an elegant bridge vaults the still waters of this captivating picture (shown on the right on page 85).

Skill level: IMPROVER/EXPERIENCED

FOR THE EMBROIDERY

14-count white Aida, 25.5 × 20 cm (10 × 8 in)

Tacking thread

Sewing needle

Embroidery frame

No 26 tapestry needle

One skein of stranded embroidery cotton (floss) in each of the colours given in the panel

FOR MOUNTING AND FRAMING

Frame with an internal aperture 17.5 × 12.5 cm (7 × 5 in)

Firm card, 17.5 × 12.5 cm (7 × 5 in)

Lightweight wadding (batting) 17.5 × 12.5 cm (7 × 5 in)

Mount, 17.5 × 12.5 cm (7 × 5 in) with an internal oval aperture 15 × 10.5 cm (6 × 4¼ in)

Solid glue stick

Strong thread for lacing

JAPANESE GARDEN PICTURE *(opposite)*

		ANCHOR	DMC	MADEIRA
−	Silver	847	3072	1709
·	Pale yellow	293	727	0110
▲	Medium yellow	305	743	0113
▢	Golden yellow	298	972	0107
▬	Orange	303	742	0114
◼	Red	29	891	0411
U	Yellow-brown	308	782	2302
↑	Brown	355	975	2303
╱	Light green	238	703	1307
+	Medium green	258	904	1413

Backstitch outline
Temple roofs and bridge: One strand of red

• These instructions are a quick-reference guide for this project. For more detailed information see Basic Techniques, page 8. For instructions on lacing, see page 11.

1. Mark the centre of the fabric with one vertical and one horizontal line of tacking (basting). Place the prepared fabric in an embroidery frame.

2. Start the embroidery in the very centre of the fabric and cross stitch the design, following the chart opposite and using two strands of embroidery cotton (floss) throughout.

3. When you have completed the cross stitching, outline the base of the bridge and the temple roofs in backstitch using one strand of red thread.

4. Remove the embroidery from the frame, hand wash if necessary (using detergent suitable for delicates) and lightly press on the wrong side with a steam iron.

5. Spread glue evenly on one side of the firm card and lightly press the wadding (batting) on top.

6. Centre the embroidery over the padded card and secure it on the back by lacing with strong thread.

7. Finally, place the padded embroidery in the frame and assemble it following the manufacturer's instructions.

THE
ℋERB
GARDEN

*The delicate scents, elegant shapes and soft colours of most garden
herbs make them a splendid addition to any garden, and when
you consider their medicinal and culinary qualities, they become even
more desirable. One of my favourite herbs is lavender, with its
fresh aroma and vibrant colour, so I devised the co-ordinated gift
set in this chapter to feature French lavender, a variety with
particularly elegant blossoms.*

The sundial's shadow is gone at noon
And the herb garden warms in the light
It is the blossoming month of June
Arrayed with Hyssops: pink, blue and white.

The sundial's shadow, stretched at sunset,
Touches the bergamot flowers
That draw in their petals, closing for rest,
While lavender bathes in the showers.

LAVENDER GIFT TAG

Project time: TWO HOURS

With its deep violet-purple flowers and soft green stems and leaves, French lavender makes a charming subject for an embroidery. This pretty gift tag is worked in just three colours.

Skill level: BEGINNER

14-count pink Aida, 7.5 cm (3 in) square (you will need more fabric if you wish to work the design in a frame)

Tacking thread

Sewing needle

No 26 tapestry needle

One skein of stranded embroidery cotton (floss) in each of the colours given in the panel

Gift tag with a 3.5 cm (1⅜ in) circular aperture

Solid glue stick

● These instructions are a quick-reference guide for this project. For more detailed information see Basic Techniques, page 8.

1. Mark the centre of the fabric with tacking (basting). This design can be worked either hand-held or placed in a frame.

2. Start the embroidery in the centre of the fabric and cross stitch the design, following the chart and using two strands of embroidery cotton (floss).

3. Outline the flowers in backstitch using one strand of dark lavender; outline the stems with one strand of light lavender.

4. When you have finished the embroidery, trim surplus material leaving a 12 mm (½ in) border all round the design. The trimmed work should be approximately 2.5 cm (1 in) larger than the aperture.

5. Spread glue evenly on the mounting flap (you can see this flap through the aperture when the card is closed). Place the embroidery in position and lightly press on the closed card to secure.

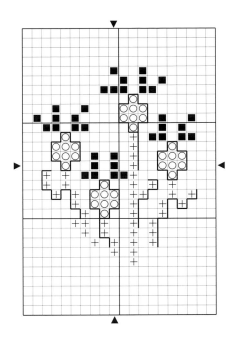

LAVENDER GIFT TAG *(left)*

		ANCHOR	DMC	MADEIRA
○	Light lavender	110	208	0804
■	Dark lavender	112	552	0713
+	Light green	214	966	1310

Backstitch outline
Flowers: One strand of dark lavender
Stems: One strand of light lavender

LAVENDER CARD & SACHET *(below)*

		ANCHOR	DMC	MADEIRA
○	Light lavender	110	208	0804
■	Dark lavender	112	552	0713
+	Light green	214	966	1310
/	Medium green	215	368	1311

Backstitch outline
Flowers: One strand of dark lavender
Stems: One strand of light lavender

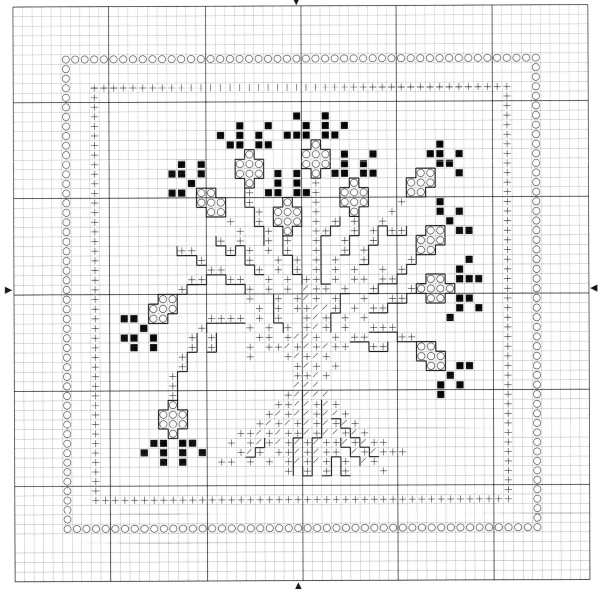

LAVENDER GREETINGS CARD

Project time: TWO DAYS

This bouquet of lavender is so lovely you'll want to frame it. Simply glue it into a ready-made card mount to make this delightful greetings card.

Skill level: BEGINNER

14-count pink Aida, 12.5 cm (5 in) square (you will need more fabric if you wish to work the embroidery in a frame)

Tacking thread

Sewing needle

No 26 tapestry needle

One skein of stranded embroidery cotton (floss) in each of the colours given in the panel

Purple ribbon bow

Card with a 7.5 cm (3 in) square aperture

Solid glue stick

● These instructions are a quick-reference guide for this project. For more detailed information see Basic Techniques, page 8.

1. Mark the centre of the fabric with one vertical and one horizontal line of tacking (basting). This design can be worked either hand-held or placed in a frame.

Below The lavender gift set comprises a pretty gift tag, the beautifully elegant card and a matching lavender-scented sachet

2. Start the embroidery in the centre and cross stitch the design, following the chart on page 91 and using two strands of thread.

3. Outline the flowers in backstitch using one strand of dark lavender; outline the stems with one strand of light lavender.

4. When you have finished the embroidery, trim surplus material leaving a 12 mm (½ in)

border all round the design. Your work should measure about 10 cm (4 in) square. Stitch the ribbon bow to the stems at the point where they are gathered in.

5. Open the card and spread glue evenly on the mounting flap (you can see this flap through the aperture when the card is closed). Place the embroidery in position and lightly press on the closed card to secure.

LAVENDER SACHET

Project time: TWO DAYS

With a sweet aroma exuding from this scented sachet, the embroidered bouquet of fresh lavender seems very real. The pretty ribbon bow completes the illusion.

Skill level: BEGINNER/IMPROVER

14-count pink Aida, 15.5 cm (6 in) square (you will need more fabric if you wish to work the embroidery in a frame)

Cotton backing fabric, 12.5 cm (5 in) square

Tacking thread

Sewing needle

No 26 tapestry needle

One skein of stranded embroidery cotton (floss) in each of the colours given in the panel

Purple ribbon bow

Sewing thread to match the Aida

Dried lavender for the filling

● **These instructions are a quick-reference guide for this project. For more detailed information see Basic Techniques, page 8.**

1. Mark the centre of the fabric with one vertical and one horizontal line of tacking (basting). This design can be worked either hand-held or placed in a frame.

2. Start the embroidery in the centre of the fabric and cross stitch the design, following the chart on page 91 and using two strands of embroidery cotton (floss).

3. Outline the flowers in backstitch using one strand of dark lavender; outline the stems with one strand of light lavender.

4. Trim surplus material leaving a 2.5 cm (1 in) border all round the design. Your work should measure 12.5 cm (5 in) square. Stitch the ribbon bow to the stems.

5. Place the embroidery and backing fabric together with right sides facing and machine a seam along three sides, taking a 12 mm (½ in) allowance. Snip the seam allowances at the corners for ease, then turn the work right sides out.

6. Lightly press the work with a steam-iron before filling with dried lavender. Turn in the open end and slip stitch it closed to finish.

BERGAMOT KEY RING

Project time: TWO DAYS

Bold pinks and fresh greens make a lively mix that is often found on Nature's palette. Here they combine in a bergamot flower which explodes outwards like a fabulous fireworks display.

Skill level: BEGINNER/IMPROVER

14-count pink Aida, 10 cm (4 in) square (you will need more fabric if you wish to work the design in a frame)

Tacking thread

Sewing needle

No 26 tapestry needle

One skein of stranded embroidery cotton (floss) in each of the colours given in the panel

Key ring with a 5 cm (2 in) square aperture

● These instructions are a quick-reference guide for this project. For more detailed information see Basic Techniques, page 8.

1. Mark the centre of the fabric with one vertical and one horizontal line of tacking (basting). This design can be worked either hand-held or placed in a frame.

2. Start the embroidery in the centre of the fabric and cross stitch the design, following the chart and using two strands of embroidery cotton (floss).

3. Outline the flower petals in backstitch using one strand of dark red embroidery cotton (floss); outline the leaves with one strand of deep pink. Work the stamens in longstitch with one strand of medium pink; use two strands of light yellow-green for the French knots.

4. Once you have finished the stitching, trim the surplus material: the fabric should measure 5 cm (2 in) square. Place the embroidery in the key ring (you may wish to insert a photograph or piece of card in the back). Finally, assemble the key ring following the manufacturer's instructions.

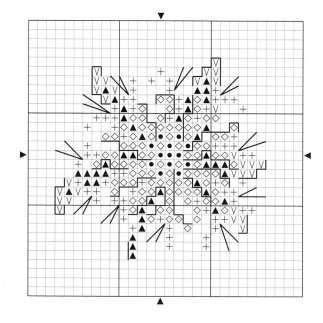

BERGAMOT KEY RING (left)

		ANCHOR	DMC	MADEIRA
+	Medium pink	31	3708	0414
◇	Deep pink	39	309	0507
V	Light yellow-green	265	3348	1501
▲	Medium yellow-green	266	3347	1502
	Dark red*	45	815	0513

*Backstitch outline
Petals: One strand of dark red
Leaves: One strand of deep pink

Longstitch
Stamens: One strand of medium pink

French knots
● Flower centre: Two strands of light yellow-green

Opposite *The bergamot key ring, card and bag threesome take only a week altogether to work*

BERGAMOT BAG

Project time: ONE WEEK

Work this lovely bergamot design on a large piece of fabric, and you can make this pretty little bag. You may want to fill it with dried herbs and hang it by the ribbon tie.

Skill level: BEGINNER/IMPROVER

14-count pink Aida, 19 x 20 cm (7½ x 8 in)

Tacking thread

Sewing needle

Embroidery frame

No 26 tapestry needle

One skein of stranded embroidery cotton (floss) in each of the colours given in the panel

Sewing thread to match the fabric

Ribbon, 6 mm (¼ in) wide and 50 cm (20 in) long

Sharp large-eyed needle for threading ribbon

● These instructions are a quick-reference guide for this project. For more detailed information see Basic Techniques, page 8.

1. Fold the fabric in half to make a rectangle 19 x 10 cm (7½ x 4 in). Unfold it and prepare to stitch the design in the right-hand section. Measure off 6 mm (¼ in) from the right-hand edge for a seam allowance and 5 cm (2 in) from the top. Then mark the centre of the remaining area with tacking (basting) as shown below left. Place the prepared fabric in a frame.

2. Start the embroidery in the centre of this section and cross stitch the design, following the chart and using two strands of thread.

3. Outline the flowers in backstitch using one strand of dark red thread; backstitch the leaves with one strand of deep pink. Work the stamens in longstitch with one strand of medium pink, then work the French knots with two strands of light yellow-green.

4. Remove the embroidery from the frame, wash if necessary, and lightly press on the wrong side with a steam iron.

5. Trim the surplus fabric so the bag measures 16 x 10 cm (6¼ x 4 in) when folded. Using matching thread, run a line of cross stitch at the top of the fabric, 6 mm (¼ in) from the edge. Remove the threads above this line to create a fringe.

6. Fold the fabric in half so the right sides are facing inwards. Machine stitch a 6 mm (¼ in) seam along the bottom and side of the bag. Overlock these seams to prevent fraying.

7. Turn the bag to the right side and lightly press it with a steam iron. Finally, insert the ribbon, working it through every fourth square with the large-eyed needle.

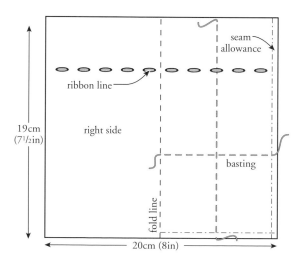

Preparing the fabric

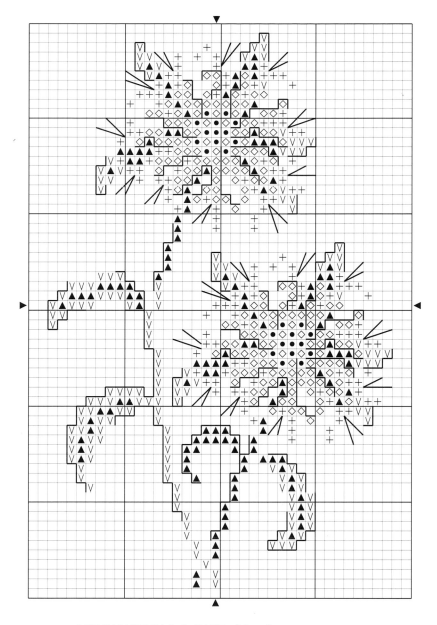

BERGAMOT BAG & CARD *(above)*

		ANCHOR	DMC	MADEIRA
+	Medium pink	31	3708	0414
◇	Deep pink	39	309	0507
V	Light yellow-green	265	3348	1501
▲	Medium yellow-green	266	3347	1502
	Dark red*	45	815	0513

*Backstitch outline
Flowers: One strand of dark red
Leaves: One strand of deep pink

Longstitch
Stamens: One strand of medium pink

French knots
● Flower centres: Two strands of light yellow-green

BERGAMOT CARD

Project time: ONE WEEK

A pair of sprightly pink bergamots pose happily on the front of this pretty greetings card. Their appearance is colourful, yet they are stitched with only four colours of thread.

Skill level: BEGINNER/IMPROVER

14-count pink Aida, 18 × 12.5 cm (7 × 5 in) – you will need more fabric if you wish to work the design in a frame

Tacking thread

Sewing needle

No 26 tapestry needle

One skein of stranded embroidery cotton (floss) in each of the colours given in the panel

A card with a 13.5 × 9 cm (5¼ × 3½ in) oval aperture

Solid glue stick

● These instructions are a quick-reference guide for this project. For more detailed information see Basic Techniques, page 8.

1. Mark the centre of the fabric with one vertical and one horizontal line of tacking (basting). This design can be worked either hand-held or placed in a frame.

2. Start the embroidery in the centre of the fabric and cross stitch the design, following the chart on page 97 and using two strands of embroidery cotton (floss).

3. Outline the flowers with backstitch using one strand of dark red thread; outline the leaves with one strand of deep pink. Work the stamens in longstitch with one strand of medium pink and use two strands of light yellow-green for the French knots.

4. When you have completed all the embroidery, trim the surplus material leaving a 12 mm (½ in) border all round the design. Your work should now measure 16.5 × 11.5 cm (6½ × 4½ in).

5. Open the card and spread glue evenly on the mounting flap (you can see this flap through the aperture when the card is closed). Position the embroidery in the card and lightly press on the closed card to secure.

HERB GARDEN PICTURE *(opposite)*

		ANCHOR	DMC	MADEIRA
·	Light beige	361	738	2013
−	Medium beige	362	436	2012
/	Brown	374	420	2009
X	Light pink	6	754	0304
▲	Medium pink	31	3708	0414
▬	Deep pink	39	309	0507
○	Medium lilac	110	208	0804
●	Dark lilac	111	552	0713
⬠	Blue	120	794	0909
I	Light yellow-green	265	3348	1501
V	Medium yellow-green	266	3347	1502
T	Dark yellow-green	267	3346	1503
╲	Light blue-green	214	368	1310
+	Medium blue-green	215	320	1311

Backstitch outline
Sundial and pedestal: One strand of brown
Lavender: One strand of dark lilac

Longstitch
Lavender stems: One strand of dark lilac

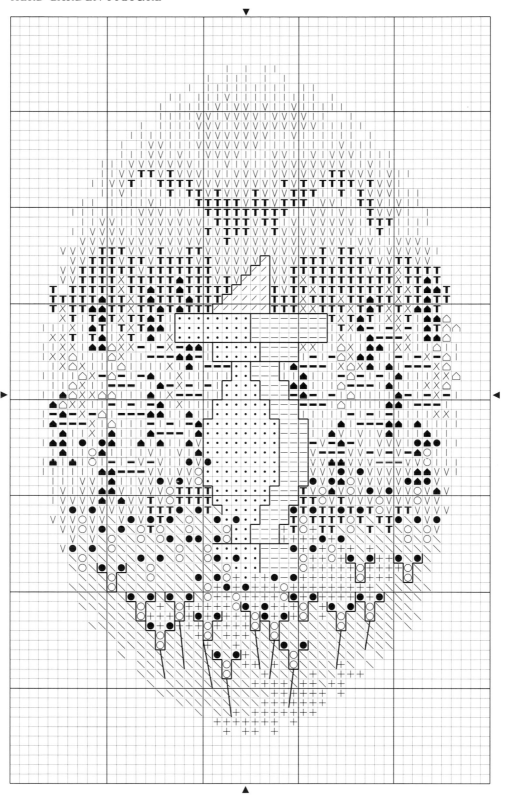

HERB GARDEN PICTURE

Project time: TWO WEEKS

In a sunny corner of the garden, brilliantly coloured lavender and bright bergamot luxuriate in the summer warmth while the sober sundial keeps watch.

Skill level: IMPROVER

FOR THE EMBROIDERY

14-count cream Aida, 25.5 × 20 cm (10 × 8 in)

Embroidery frame

Tacking thread

Sewing needle

No 26 tapestry needle

One skein of stranded embroidery cotton (floss) in each of the colours given in the panel

FOR MOUNTING AND FRAMING

Frame with a 17.5 × 12.5 cm (7 × 5 in) internal aperture

Firm card, 17.5 × 12.5 cm (7 × 5 in)

Lightweight wadding (batting), 17.5 × 12.5 cm (7 × 5 in)

Mount, 17.5 × 12.5 cm (7 × 5 in) with a 13 × 9 cm (5¼ × 3½ in) internal oval aperture

Solid glue stick

Strong thread for lacing

● These instructions are a quick-reference guide for this project. For more detailed information see Basic Techniques, page 8. For instructions on lacing, see page 11.

1. Mark the centre of the fabric with one vertical and one horizontal line of tacking (basting). Place the prepared fabric in an embroidery frame.

2. Start the embroidery in the centre of the fabric and cross stitch the design, following the chart on page 99 and using two strands of embroidery cotton (floss).

3. Outline the sundial and pedestal in backstitch with one strand of brown thread; outline the lavender with one strand of dark lilac. Then work the lavender stems in longstitch with one strand of dark lilac.

4. Remove the embroidery from the frame, wash if necessary, and lightly press on the wrong side with a steam iron.

5. Spread glue evenly on one side of the firm card and lightly press the wadding (batting) on top. Centre the embroidery over the padded card and secure with lacing.

6. Finally, assemble the frame following the manufacturer's instructions.

THE
*T*ROPICAL
GARDEN

Tropical plants require a particular climate to grow outside, but with a conservatory anyone can now grow them indoors. Many of the plants that thrive in our homes are from the tropics anyway, and I have decided to feature one of our most common house plants – the cactus. As well as small domestic cacti I am showing the large desert cacti which burst into colour in the rainy season.

*Winter winds ripple the white sand
'Til spring-time rains moisten the land.
Then the cactus plants flower at last
Where the palm tree's shadow is cast.*

*Gazania petals flame in sunset reds,
Gently nodding their daisy-shaped heads.
Majestic above them proteas have grown,
Fluttering great petals of orange and brown.*

CACTUS GIFT TAG

Project time: TWO HOURS

A cactus asks for very little – minimum water and feeding – but it gives a lot in return, bursting into bloom with the least encouragement. It makes a charming subject for this gift tag.

Skill level: BEGINNER

14-count white Aida, 7.5 cm (3 in) square (you will need more fabric if you wish to work the embroidery in a frame)

Tacking thread

Sewing needle

No 26 tapestry needle

One skein of stranded embroidery cotton (floss) in each of the colours given in the panel

Gift tag with a 3.5 cm (1⅜ in) square aperture

Solid glue stick

● These instructions are a quick-reference guide for this project. For more detailed information see Basic Techniques, page 8.

1. Mark the centre of the fabric with one vertical and one horizontal line of tacking (basting). This design can be worked either hand-held or placed in a frame.

2. Start the embroidery in the centre of the fabric and cross stitch the design, following the chart on page 107 and using two strands of embroidery cotton (floss).

3. Outline the cactus in backstitch using one strand of dark green; to outline the pot use one strand of dark brown. Work the French knots for the flower centres with one strand of yellow.

4. When you have finished the embroidery, trim surplus material leaving a 12 mm (½ in) border all round the design. The trimmed work should be approximately 2.5 cm (1 in) larger than the aperture on the gift tag.

5. Spread glue evenly on the mounting flap (you can see this through the aperture when the tag is closed). Place the embroidery in position and lightly press the closed tag to secure the embroidery.

Above This prickly trio of tag, picture and card make up the tropical gift set.

CACTUS PICTURE

Project time: TWO DAYS

The bold red and green colours of this thriving cactus ensure it is an especially cheering gift.

Skill level: BEGINNER

14-count white Aida, 12.5 cm (5 in) square (you will need more fabric if you wish to work the design in a frame)

Tacking thread

Sewing needle

No 26 tapestry needle

One skein of stranded embroidery cotton (floss) in each of the colours given in the panel

Miniature frame with a 5 cm (2 in) square aperture

● These instructions are a quick-reference guide for this project. For more detailed information see Basic Techniques, page 8.

1. Mark the centre of the fabric with one vertical and one horizontal line of tacking (basting). This design can be worked either hand-held or placed in a frame.

2. Start the embroidery in the centre of the fabric and cross stitch the design, following the chart and using two strands of thread.

3. Outline the cactus in backstitch using one strand of dark green; use one strand of dark brown to backstitch round the pot. Work French knots for the flower centres with one strand of yellow.

4. When you have finished the embroidery, trim surplus material. Your work should measure 5 cm (2 in) square. Place the picture in the frame and secure the back.

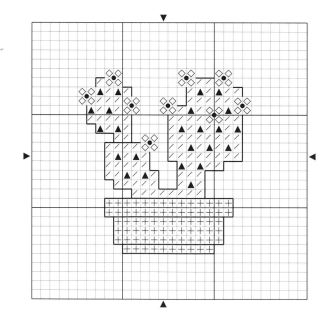

CACTUS PICTURE *(left)*, GIFT TAG *(right)* & GREETINGS CARD *(far right)*

		ANCHOR	DMC	MADEIRA
◇	Orange	316	740	0203
▲	Light green	254	704	1308
/	Medium green	255	906	1410
+	Light brown	355	975	2303
	Dark green*	258	904	1413
	Dark brown*	360	898	2006
	Yellow**	289	972	0107

*Backstitch outline
Cactus: One strand of dark green
Pot: One strand of dark brown

**French knots
● Flower centres: One strand of yellow

CACTUS GREETINGS CARD

Project time: TWO DAYS

There's something very engaging about the simple, knobbly shape of a cactus that makes it a very pleasing image. This one is particularly appealing.

Skill level: BEGINNER

14-count white Aida, 12.5 (5 in) square (you will need more fabric if you wish to work the design in a frame)

Tacking thread

Sewing needle

No 26 tapestry needle

One skein of stranded embroidery cotton (floss) in each of the colours given in the panel

A card with a 6.5 cm (2½ in) square aperture

Solid glue stick

● These instructions are a quick-reference guide for this project. For more detailed information see Basic Techniques, page 8.

1. Mark the centre of the fabric with tacking (basting). This design can be worked either hand-held or placed in a frame.

2. Start the embroidery in the centre of the fabric and cross stitch the design, following the chart and using two strands of thread.

3. Outline the cactus in backstitch using one strand of dark green; use one strand of dark brown to backstitch round the pot. Work French knots for the flower centres with one strand of yellow.

4. When you have finished the embroidery, trim surplus material leaving a 6 mm (¼ in) border all round the design. Your work should measure 8 cm (3¼ in) square.

5. Open the card and spread glue evenly on the mounting flap (you can see this flap through the aperture when the card is closed). Place the embroidery in position and lightly press on the closed card to secure it.

CACTUS GREETINGS CARD

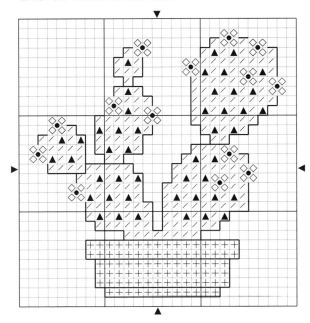

CACTUS GIFT TAG

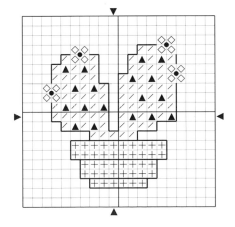

COLOURFUL FLOWER PICTURES

Project time: TWO DAYS (PROTEA); ONE WEEK (GAZANIAS)

In bold brown, red, orange and cream, a bright protea makes the perfect companion
for flame-coloured gazanias which worship the sun with their petals.

Skill level: BEGINNER/IMPROVER

14-count white Aida, 15 cm (6 in) square for the protea picture and 20 cm (8 in) square for the gazanias

Tacking thread and sewing needle

Embroidery frame

No 26 tapestry needle

One skein of stranded embroidery cotton (floss) in each of the colours given in the panel

White felt for the backing, 10 cm (4 in) square for the protea picture and 12.5 cm (5 in) square for the gazanias

Circular flexi-frames, 6.5 cm (2½ in) and 10 cm (4 in) across

White sewing cotton

Strong thread for lacing

● These instructions are a quick-reference guide for this project. For more detailed information see Basic Techniques, page 8.

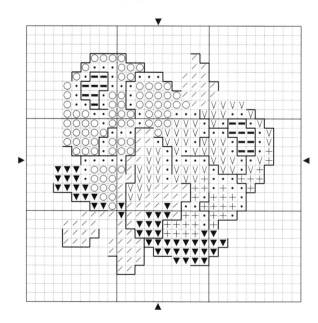

1. Decide which of the two designs you are going to work first. Mark the centre of the appropriate fabric square with one vertical and one horizontal line of tacking (basting). Place the prepared fabric in an embroidery frame.

2. Start the first embroidery in the centre of the fabric and cross stitch the design, following the chart for the protea (below left) or gazanias (page 110). Use two strands of embroidery cotton (floss).

3. Outline the protea or gazania flowers in backstitch with one strand of dark red; to outline the protea leaves use one strand of dark green. Work French knots for the gazania flower centres using three strands of light green or medium green. Now work the second design.

4. Remove each picture from its embroidery frame. Wash if necessary and press lightly, before mounting each centrally in its frame.

FLOWERING PROTEA *(left)*

		ANCHOR	DMC	MADEIRA
·	Cream	275	712	2101
/	Light green	255	907	1410
▼	Medium green	256	906	1411
V	Deep orange	332	608	0205
+	Red	333	606	0206
▬	Dark red	20	304	0407
○	Brown	340	355	0401
	Dark green*	258	904	1413

Backstitch outline
Flower: One strand of dark red
Leaves: One strand of dark green

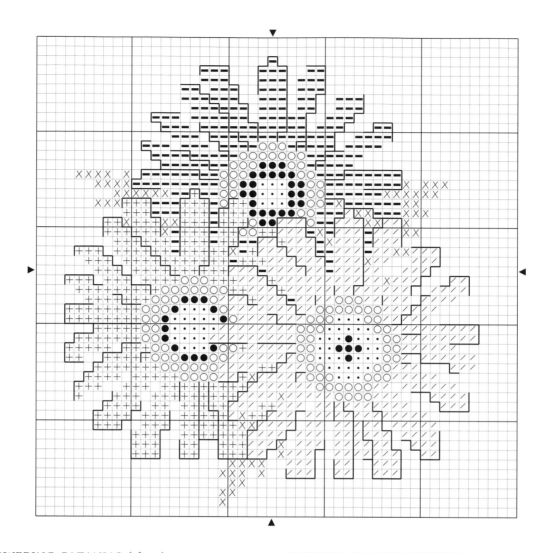

FLOWERING GAZANIAS *(above)*

		ANCHOR	DMC	MADEIRA
/	Orange	316	740	0203
+	Orange-red	332	608	0205
▬	Red	334	606	0206
○	Dark red	20	304	0407
✕	Medium green	255	907	1410
	Light green*	254	704	1308

Backstitch outline
Flowers: One strand of dark red

*French knots
·	Flower centres: Three strands of light green
●	Flower centres: Three strands of medium green

TROPICAL GARDEN PICTURE *(right)*

		ANCHOR	DMC	MADEIRA
╲	Cream	275	712	2101
/	Pale green	254	704	1308
T	Light green	255	907	1410
▬	Medium green	256	906	1411
■	Dark green	258	904	1413
◇	Orange	316	740	0203
+	Orange-red	332	608	0205
V	Red	334	606	0206
△	Dark red	19	321	0211

Backstitch outline
Cacti and leaves: One strand of dark green
Flowers: One strand of dark red

French knots
●	Flower centres: Two strands of cream

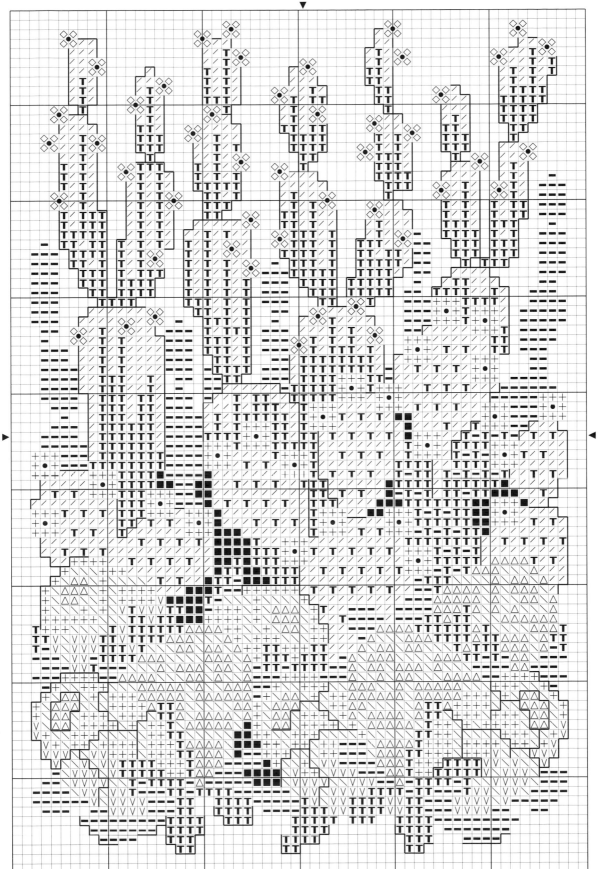

TROPICAL GARDEN PICTURE

Project time: TWO WEEKS

*Rugged cactus spires rise out of the parched earth, layer upon layer, and burst into bloom
in celebration of the rains. The flaming blooms transform the plants into the beauties of the desert.*

Skill level: IMPROVER/EXPERIENCED

FOR THE EMBROIDERY

14-count white Aida, 25.5 x 20 cm (10 x 8 in)

Tacking thread

Sewing needle

Embroidery frame

No 26 tapestry needle

One skein of stranded embroidery cotton (floss)
in each of the colours given in the panel

FOR MOUNTING AND FRAMING

Frame with a 17.5 x 12.5 cm (7 x 5 in) internal
aperture

Firm card, 17.5 x 12.5 cm (7 x 5 in)

Lightweight wadding (batting), 17.5 x 12.5 cm
(7 x 5 in)

Solid glue stick

Strong thread for lacing

● These instructions are a quick-reference guide
for this project. For more detailed information see
Basic Techniques, page 8. For instructions on
lacing see Basic Techniques, page 11.

1. Mark the centre of the fabric with one
vertical and one horizontal line of tacking

(basting). Mount the prepared fabric in an
embroidery frame.

2. Start the embroidery in the centre of the
fabric and cross stitch the design, following
the chart on page 111 and using two strands
of embroidery cotton (floss).

3. When you have finished the cross
stitching, outline the cacti and leaves in
backstitch with one strand of dark green;
outline the flowers with one strand of dark
red. Work the French knots for the flower
centres with two strands of cream.

4. Remove the embroidery from the frame,
wash if necessary, and lightly press on the
wrong side with a steam iron.

5. Spread the glue evenly on one side of the
firm card and lightly press the wadding
(batting) on top.

6. Centre the embroidery over the padded
card and secure it with lacing.

7. Finally, assemble the frame following the
manufacturer's instructions.

THE
ROSE
GARDEN

*A rose garden, for me, always creates a feeling of tranquillity,
and I have tried to create that feeling of peace in my Rose Garden
Picture. The rose as a flower, however, I associate with romance
and romantic celebrations such as engagements, weddings
and wedding anniversaries. The golden yellow rose designs, for
example, would be ideal for a golden wedding celebration; and you can
easily change its colour.*

Hidden from the rushing world,
My garden's secret is unfurled.
There my roses tranquil grow
From urns and cluster round below.

Blossoms in the breezes blow,
In shades of red and peach they grow;
And pale flowers cool the tone
As I wander in joy all alone.

ROSEBUD GIFT TAG

Project time: TWO HOURS

Take one perfect rosebud and transform a plain white gift tag into something special.

Skill level: BEGINNER

14-count mint Aida, 7.5 cm (3 in) square (you will need more fabric if you wish to work the design in a frame)

Tacking thread and needle

No 26 tapestry needle

One skein of stranded embroidery cotton (floss) in each of the colours given in the panel

Gift tag with a 3.5 cm (1½ in) aperture

Solid glue stick

● **These instructions are a quick-reference guide for the project. You will find more detailed information in Basic Techniques, page 8.**

1. Mark the centre of the fabric with one vertical and one horizontal line of tacking (basting). This design can be worked either hand-held or placed in a frame.

2. Start working the embroidery in the centre of the fabric and cross stitch the design by following the chart and using two strands of thread.

3. Outline the rosebud by backstitching using one strand of plum thread.

4. When you have finished the embroidery, trim surplus material leaving a 12 mm (½ in) border round the design. Your trimmed work should be approximately 2.5 cm (1 in) larger than the aperture.

5. Open up the tag and spread glue evenly on the mounting flap (you can see this flap through the aperture when the card is closed). Carefully place the embroidery in position and lightly press the work and the front of the card to secure.

ROSEBUD HANDKERCHIEF

Project time: TWO HOURS

Lace and roses are an irresistible combination. Teamed with fine cotton lawn,
they make the most delicate of gifts. This is an excellent project for beginners who want
to learn how to use waste canvas.

Skill level: BEGINNER/IMPROVER

Cream cotton handkerchief (any size)*

14-count waste canvas, 5 cm (2 in) square

Sharp pointed needle and pins

One skein of stranded embroidery cotton (floss) in each of the colours given in the panel

Tweezers for removing waste canvas threads

*I couldn't find a cream handkerchief so I made one. If you have the same difficulty you can also make one. You will need a 23 cm (9 in) square of cotton fabric and sufficient lace to trim the edges. Overlock the edges by machine and stitch the lace trim to the edge to finish the handkerchief.

● These instructions are a quick-reference guide for this project. You will find more detailed information in Basic Techniques, page 8. See page 11 for instructions on using waste canvas.

1. Place the waste canvas on the right side of the handkerchief, about 12 mm (½ in) from the corner, so that the design will point to the corner, and pin the canvas in position. Once you have worked enough stitches to secure the canvas to the napkin, you can remove the pins.

2. Start the embroidery in the centre of the canvas and cross stitch using three strands of thread in a sharp pointed needle. Stitch carefully to make sure that you do not split the threads of the waste canvas.

3. Outline the rosebud in backstitch using two strands of plum thread.

4. Dab the waste canvas with a damp sponge. Carefully remove all the canvas threads with tweezers.

5. When all threads have been removed, wash the work if necessary, and lightly press on the wrong side with a steam iron.

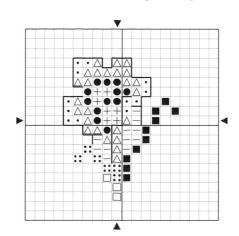

ROSEBUD TAG AND HANDKERCHIEF *(left)*

		ANCHOR	DMC	MADEIRA
·	Lemon yellow	292	3078	0102
△	Orange yellow	313	742	2301
+	Orange pink	328	3341	0301
−	Deep pink	11	350	0213
●	Plum	59	600	0704
⁚⁚	Light green	243	912	1213
☐	Medium green	244	911	1214
■	Dark green	246	699	1304

Backstitch outline
Rosebud on gift tag: One strand of plum
Rosebud on handkerchief: Two strands of plum

ROSE GREETINGS CARD

Project time: TWO DAYS

Delicate sprays of roses worked on a cool mint-green background make an elegant greetings card for almost any occasion.

Skill level: BEGINNER/IMPROVER

14-count mint Aida, 12.5 cm (5 in) square
(you will need more fabric if you wish to work the design in a frame)

Tacking thread and needle

No 26 tapestry needle

One skein of stranded embroidery cotton (floss) in each of the colours given in the panel

A card with a 7.5 cm (3 in) square aperture

Solid glue stick

Frame (optional)

● These instructions are a quick-reference guide for this project. You will find more detailed information in Basic Techniques, page 8.

1. Mark the centre of the fabric with one vertical and one horizontal line of tacking (basting). This design can be worked either hand-held or placed in a frame.

Below Worked as a gift set, the greetings card, gift tag and handkerchief become a one week project

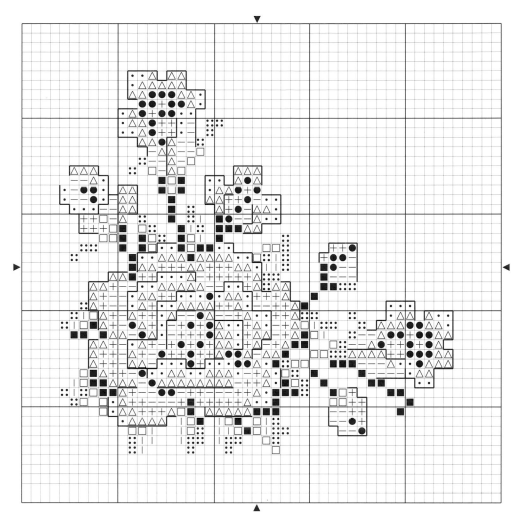

2. Start the embroidery in the centre of the fabric and cross stitch the design, following the chart and using two strands of thread.

3. Outline the roses in backstitch using one strand of plum thread.

4. When you have finished the embroidery, trim surplus material leaving a 12 mm (½ in) border round the design. Your trimmed work should measure 10 cm (4 in) square.

5. Open up the card and spread glue evenly on the mounting flap (this can be seen through the aperture when the card is closed). Place the embroidery in position and lightly press on the closed card to stick the embroidery to the card.

ROSE GREETINGS CARD

		ANCHOR	DMC	MADEIRA
·	Lemon yellow	292	3078	0102
△	Orange-yellow	313	742	2301
+	Orange-pink	328	3341	0301
−	Deep pink	11	350	0213
●	Plum	59	600	0704
|	Pale green	241	955	1211
∷	Light green	243	912	1213
□	Medium green	244	911	1214
■	Dark green	246	699	1304

Backstitch outline
Flowers: One strand of plum

ROSE NAPKIN

Project time: TWO DAYS

Create a unique place setting by working roses on a napkin that matches the table mat. Why not carry on and work a complete set of your own special table linen, dressing your table to stunning effect?

Skill level: EXPERIENCED

Cotton napkin (any size)

14-count waste canvas, 10 x 7.5 cm (4 x 3 in)

Sharp pointed needle and pins

One skein of stranded embroidery cotton (floss) in each of the colours given in the panel

Tweezers for removing waste canvas threads

• **These instructions are a quick-reference guide for this project. You will find more detailed information in Basic Techniques, page 8. See page 11 for instructions on using waste canvas.**

1. Pin the waste canvas to the right side of the napkin so that the design will point to the corner. Remove the pins after you have taken a few stitches.

2. Start the embroidery in the centre of the canvas and cross stitch the design following the chart on page 122 and using three strands of thread in a sharp pointed needle. Stitch carefully to make sure that you do not split the threads of the waste canvas.

3. Outline the flowers in backstitch using two strands of plum thread.

4. Dab the waste canvas with a damp sponge. Carefully remove all the canvas threads with tweezers.

ROSE TABLE MAT

Project time: ONE WEEK

Waste canvas lets you work these enchanting rambling roses on closely woven fabrics such as this table mat. The green mat used here is a lovely foil for the delicate pink roses.

Skill level: EXPERIENCED

A cotton table mat with a side measurement of 33 cm (13 in)

14-count waste canvas, 33 x 7.5 cm (13 x 3 in)

Sharp pointed needle, pins and ordinary sewing cotton

One skein of stranded embroidery cotton (floss) in each of the colours given in the panel

Tweezers for removing waste canvas threads

• **These instructions are a quick-reference guide for this project. You will find more detailed information in Basic Techniques, page 8. See page 11 for instructions on using waste canvas.**

1. Pin the waste canvas to the right side of the table mat in position. Secure it to the table mat with a line of tacking (basting).

Opposite The matching rose table mat and napkin

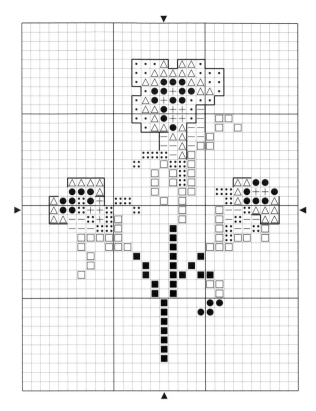

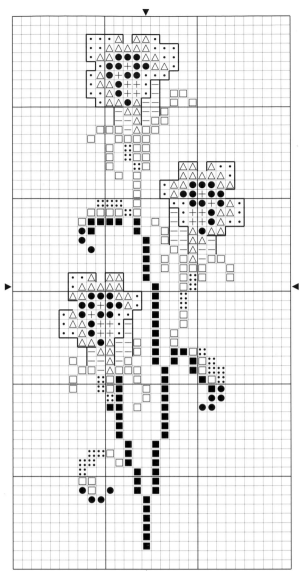

ROSE NAPKIN *(above)* & TABLE MAT *(right)*

		ANCHOR	DMC	MADEIRA
·	Lemon yellow	292	3078	0102
△	Orange-yellow	313	742	2301
+	Orange-pink	328	3341	0301
−	Deep pink	11	350	0213
●	Plum	59	600	0704
∷	Light green	243	912	1213
▢	Medium green	244	911	1214
■	Dark green	246	699	1304

Backstitch outline
Flowers: Two strands of plum

2. Start the embroidery in the centre of the canvas and cross stitch the design using three strands of thread. Stitch carefully to make sure that you do not split the threads of the waste canvas.

3. Outline the flowers in backstitch using two strands of plum thread.

4. Dab the waste canvas with a damp sponge to release the size. Carefully remove all the canvas threads.

ROSE GARDEN PICTURE *(opposite)*

		ANCHOR	DMC	MADEIRA
·	Lemon yellow	292	3078	0102
−	Mustard	874	834	2203
∷	Orange-yellow	313	742	2301
+	Orange-pink	328	3341	0301
−	Deep pink	11	350	0213
●	Plum	59	600	0704
		Pale green	241	955	1211
V	Light green	243	912	1213
▢	Medium green	244	911	1214
■	Dark green	246	699	1304

Backstitch outline
Urn and pedestal: One strand of dark green
Flowers: One strand of plum

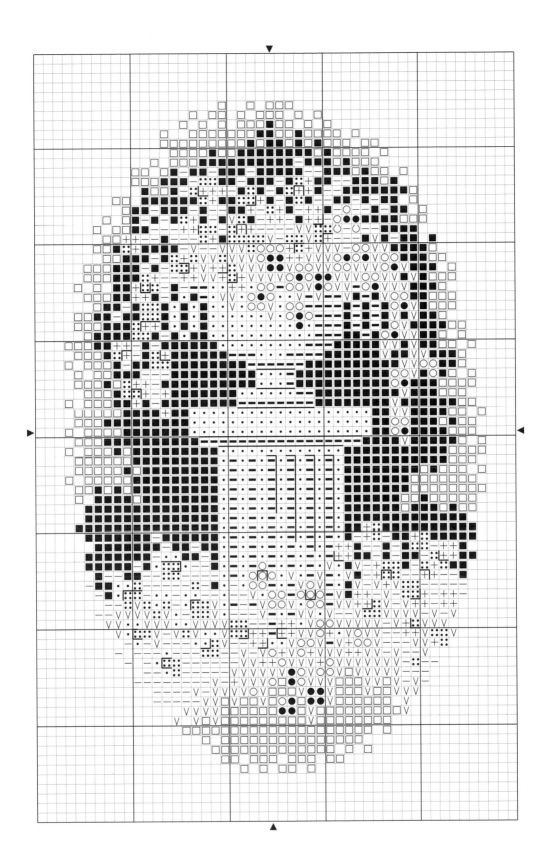

ROSE GARDEN PICTURE

Project time: TWO WEEKS

Tumbling roses cascade downwards, reaching towards a cloud of beautiful blooms at the base of the picture. The warmth and movement of these lovely flowers make a pleasing contrast to the lines of the urn and pedestal.

Skill level: IMPROVER

FOR THE EMBROIDERY

14-count mint Aida, 25.5 × 20 cm (10 × 8 in)

Tacking thread and needle

No 26 tapestry needle

One skein of stranded embroidery cotton (floss) in each of the colours given in the panel

Embroidery frame

FOR MOUNTING AND FRAMING

One piece of firm card, 17.5 × 12.5 cm (7 × 5 in)

One piece of lightweight wadding (batting), 17.5 × 12.5 cm (7 × 5 in)

Mount, 17.5 × 12.5 cm (7 × 5 in), with an internal oval aperture of 13 × 9 cm (5$\frac{1}{8}$ × 3$\frac{1}{2}$ in)

Solid glue stick

Strong thread for lacing

● These instructions are a quick-reference guide for this project. You will find more detailed information in Basic Techniques, page 8.

1. Mark the centre of the fabric with one vertical and one horizontal line of tacking (basting). Place the fabric in a frame.

2. Start the embroidery in the centre of the fabric and cross stitch the design, following the chart on page 123 and using two strands of embroidery cotton (floss).

3. Outline the urn and pedestal in backstitch using one strand of dark green thread; outline the roses in backstitch using one strand of plum thread.

4. Remove the embroidery from the frame, hand wash if necessary (using a detergent suitable for delicates), and lightly press on the wrong side with a steam iron.

5. Spread the glue evenly on one side of the card and attach the wadding (batting) by lightly pressing it on the sticky surface.

6. Centre the embroidery over the padded card and secure by lacing the edges together with strong thread on the back.

7. Finally, assemble the frame following the manufacturer's instructions.

Opposite The delightful rose garden picture

ACKNOWLEDGEMENTS

My grateful thanks go to my husband Robert for his
invaluable help and to my daughter Elizabeth for her poems
and beautiful stitching.

I would also like to thank Coats Crafts UK for the
threads and fabric used in this book, and
Framecraft Miniatures for all the supplementary items for
making up the projects.

My thanks also to Knight and Lee of Southsea who supplied
the props for the photographs.

LIST OF SUPPLIERS

Coats Crafts UK
McMullen Road
Darlington
Co. Durham DL1 1YQ
Telephone 01325 381010

DMC Creative World Ltd
62 Pullman Road
Wigston,
Leicester, LE8 2DY
Telephone 0116 2811040

Madeira Threads UK Ltd
Thirsk Industrial Park
York Road, Thirsk
N.Yorkshire Y07 3BX
Telephone 01845 524880

Framecraft Miniatures Ltd
372/376 Summer Lane
Hockley
Birmingham B19 3QA
Telephone 0121 212 0551

INDEX